Lampton Road -
Hounslow Central.

REAL WORSHIP   27/7/92

31 Bath Road.   The Gospel Hall.
                Hounslow,
Lord's Day   Sunday
Breaking of Bread. 11-am-
Sunday School. 3.30pm
Gospel Meeting   6-30 pm
Monday.

Prayer Meeting.   8 pm.

Wednesday.

Bible Reading 7. 45 pm.

Real Worship

WARREN WIERSBE

KINGSWAY PUBLICATIONS
EASTBOURNE

ISBN 0 86065 487 7

Printed in Great Britain for
KINGSWAY PUBLICATIONS LTD
Lottbridge Drove, Eastbourne, E. Sussex BN23 6NT by
Cox & Wyman Ltd, Reading.

To our choice friend

DON WYRTZEN

who combines theological truth
with technical excellence
and enriches the church with music
that glorifies God.
My wife and I have been greatly blessed
by his friendship and ministry,
and we want to say,
"Thank you!"

CONTENTS

IV. WORSHIP INVOLVES WARFARE

PART I

Invitation to Worship

Religion is that which binds a man. Every man is bound somewhere, somehow, to a throne, to a government, to an authority, to something that is supreme, to something to which he offers sacrifice, and burns incense, and bends the knee.

G. CAMPBELL MORGAN[1]

CHAPTER 1 *In which the author admits his frustration*

YOU MUST UNDERSTAND from the beginning that the writing of this book has been a frustrating experience for me.

At first, I blamed my frustration on the breadth of the subject; and I wondered if *any* writer was capable of dealing with so vast a theme as Christian worship. Beside that, certain aspects of worship are not easy to define or explain; and at times I felt like a man trying to lay sunbeams in a row while evening was marching in.

Then I decided that the problem was not the vastness of the subject but the narrowness of my own experience. After all, most of my worship experience has been in the fundamentalist "independent church" tradition where the word *worship* was found only on the cover of the hymnal. If not by word, at least by example, my peers taught me to be suspicious of "liturgy" and to major on winning the lost and sending out foreign missionaries. Even my ministerial training added little to my appreciation of Christian worship.

Imagine my surprise years later when I discovered that *every* church followed a liturgy—either a good one or a bad one—and that I could learn a great deal about the worship of God from churches that I had excluded from my fellowship. What a rude awakening!

In recent years I have shared worship experiences in many varied settings: mission stations and churches in Africa, South America, Central America, and Europe; English cathedrals; Brethren assemblies; churches of one denomination or another across the United States and Canada; house churches; camps and conferences; and even a few denominational conventions. At the same time, I have been closely studying the lives and ministries of the great preachers and missionaries of the evangelical tradition, people as far apart on the religious spectrum as Charles Haddon Spurgeon and John Henry

Newman; and I think I have developed a sympathy with and an appreciation for what is best in their ministries.

Believe me, it was not easy! More than once I longed for those days of comfort and security when all truth was safely tucked into my notebook, every question was answered, and every Christian was accurately identified and pigeonholed. The writing of this book has reopened old wounds in my heart, recalled painful growth experiences, and forced me to find the courage to say what I think needs to be said, even though some of my best friends might disagree with me.

No, this book is not a "spiritual autopsy" in which I confess my past ministerial faults and announce that I am making some dramatic theological or ecclesiastical change. I still hold to the fundamentals of the faith, and I plan to continue to worship in the "free church" tradition. *But I want to enrich my experience of spiritual worship, both in my private devotions and in congregational service.* And I want to be able to appreciate the worship experiences of my brothers and sisters in Christ, even though we may have our minor differences when it comes to matters liturgical.

In fact, you and I may disagree on some aspects of Christian doctrine, but I am sure there is one thing we definitely agree on: *You and I personally, and the church collectively, are desperately in need of transformation.* We are weary of "business as usual." We need and want a transforming experience from the Lord, the kind of spiritual visitation that will help to heal our broken homes and our split churches; that will strip away our religious veneer and get us back to reality; that will restore true spiritual values and destroy the cheap counterfeits we have been foisting on ourselves and the lost world; that will, most of all, bring such glory to God that the world will sit up and take notice and confess that "God is truly among you" (1 Cor. 14:25).

I love the church. I have devoted nearly a quarter of a century to pastoral ministry in three churches. In my present ministry, I often speak to local congregations, pastors' conferences, and denominational meetings of one kind or another. My wife and I have tried to be faithful members of the local church where we hold our membership. In my preaching and writing ministry, I have attempted to encourage pastors and church leaders and to emphasize the importance of the church.

However, my love for the church has not made me blind to her spots and wrinkles. I have no intention of listing here all the things that are wrong with our churches today: it would be too painful for me and not too profitable for you. Churches are made up of people like you and me; and we both know that churches cannot change until the people change—until you and I are transformed by the Spirit of God to become more like the Son of God. Two statements from Paul keep coming to mind, statements that I have turned into prayers for my own life.

> But we all, with unveiled face, beholding as in a mirror the glory of the Lord, are being transformed into the same image from glory to glory, just as by the Spirit of the Lord. (2 Cor. 3:18)

> And do not be conformed to this world, but be transformed by the renewing of your mind, that you may prove what is that good and acceptable and perfect will of God. (Rom. 12:2)

I sincerely believe that the transforming experience Paul wrote about is the result of the right kind of personal and corporate worship. We have tried everything else. Now it is time that we returned to God's way and tried worship.

SUBSTITUTES FOR WORSHIP

You and I have watched the religious trends over the years, and we have been alternately encouraged and discouraged. In the early years of my ministry, I was told that *separation* was the secret of a successful church; but then I saw "separated churches" fight among themselves, split and splinter, and sometimes hurt the testimony of Christ in a community. While I believe in biblical separation, I do not believe that it is a source of spiritual blessing *unless* it is the by-product of true spiritual worship. It is not enough to "cleanse ourselves from all filthiness of the flesh and spirit" if we are not "perfecting holiness in the fear of God" (2 Cor. 7:1). Separation apart from worship can become (and usually does become) a brittle piety that breeds arrogance, legalism, and an isolation from both the world and the church that, in my thinking, is not biblical.

Then I was told that *evangelism* was the main thing. If each church member would only start witnessing and winning the lost, our churches would be transformed. So, we began to teach classes on soul-winning and to structure our public services so that it was easy for the unsaved to "make a decision for Christ."

In the midst of directing one of these programs, I was asked by a discerning church officer, "Pastor, if God gives us any converts, is our church ready to take them in? I mean, do we have the kind of spiritual atmosphere that will encourage them to grow?"

Another rude awakening! I began to realize that evangelism divorced from true worship can become merely a program tacked on to an already overloaded ecclesiastical machine, or, even worse, a struggle for statistics and "results." Isaiah became an evangelist *after* attending a worship service in the temple and seeing God "high and lifted up" (Isa. 6:1). Evangelism is an essential part of the church's ministry, but it must be the result of worship, or it will not glorify God.

No sooner did the evangelism fad start to fade when somebody suggested that *missions* was the key to a spiritual church. We were admonished to preach missions, to give more and more to missions, and to challenge our people to go out themselves into the whitened harvest-fields of the world. But nobody explained to us that missions, like separation and evangelism, must be a product of worship; otherwise it is only a new gimmick to motivate the church, and the motivation will not last.

In one sense, Abraham was the first foreign missionary named in the Bible. He was told to leave his home and go to a distant and unknown land, and there to bear witness for the true and living God. How did this missionary venture begin? "The God of glory appeared to our father Abraham," explained Stephen (Acts 7:2). It sounds a good deal like Isaiah's experience! In fact, it is worth noting that even Paul's missionary call came to him while he was sharing in worship in the church at Antioch. "As they ministered to the Lord and fasted, the Holy Spirit said, 'Now separate to Me Barnabas and Saul for the work to which I have called them'" (Acts 13:2). The Greek word translated "ministered" is *leitourgeō* and refers to priestly service rendered to God (see Heb. 10:11). Paul was probably praying, fasting, and worshiping God when the summons came.

When missions is divorced from worship, the human need can

become more important than the divine glory; and the strategy used might be the result of man's observations rather than a God-given spiritual vision. It is when we worship God that we discover afresh that His thoughts and ways are far above ours.

"And what more shall I say? For the time would fail me to tell of" Sunday school contests, bus ministries, youth rallies, discipleship programs, church-growth seminars, liturgical renewal movements, ecumenical programs, and denominational promotions, all of which promised new life for me and my congregation, but none of which really did the job. Why? Because they were cut flowers that had no roots; they had been divorced from worship and therefore could not produce fruit.

Please do not misunderstand me: many of these things are good and important to the local church, but they are not good in themselves. They are good only if they are a by-product of spiritual worship. This explains why success in these ventures often creates more problems than it solves; for the emphasis is on man's techniques and achievements, not on God's power and glory. "In whatever man does without God," wrote George MacDonald, "he must fail miserably—or succeed more miserably." The church today is starting to suffer from success, and it is time we returned to worship.

INVITATION TO A PILGRIMAGE

I discovered a surprising thing as I wrote this book: worship is at the center of everything that the church believes, practices, and seeks to accomplish. In order to understand worship, I must understand God, God's creation, myself, the church, and the ministry I am trying to fulfill. This book has been a "spiritual catalyst" for me. It has forced me to examine and evaluate my own spiritual life and the priorities that help to direct it. No doubt that is where some of the frustration has come in. It is not easy to admit wrong thinking and wrong serving!

I have experienced a growing vision of the greatness of God, not as dramatic as the vision Isaiah had in the temple, but a blessed experience just the same. My Bible shines with new light. I am no longer analyzing texts in order to organize sermons; I am meeting God in His

Word and discovering the reality of a song I have sung often but little understood:

> Beyond the sacred page, I seek Thee, Lord;
> My spirit pants for Thee, O living Word!
>   MARY A. LATHBURY

I have learned that preaching is an act of worship and that my message must be a sacrifice placed on the altar to the glory of God.

Not only has God become more real and the Bible more exciting, but all the things God wants me to do have become joyfully more natural: praying, witnessing, loving the brethren (even those who disagree with me!), giving, ministering, helping others bear their burdens, handling interruptions, caring for my body, and worshiping with God's people. To be sure, I still fail and often have to struggle; but this new emphasis on worship has begun to take the strain out of the Christian life.

I even find myself interrupting what I am doing and just lifting my heart in worship to God. Sometimes I even lift my hands as well! And there are times in public worship when I stop singing, bow my head, and (sometimes with tears) just worship the Father in heaven. Have I seen any "special results" in my ministry? No, but I must leave that with God. I am not worshiping Him because of what He will do for me, but because of what He is to me. When worship becomes pragmatic, it ceases to be worship. R. G. LeTourneau used to say, "If you give because it pays, it won't pay." That principle applies to worship: if you worship because it pays, it won't pay. Our motive must be to please God and glorify Him alone.

As you walk with me through the pages of this book, you will be sharing my personal pilgrimage as I have rediscovered worship and the transforming power it can bring to our lives and our churches, to the glory of God. At some points in our pilgrimage, you and I may disagree; and I welcome this, because we must be honest with ourselves and with each other. All I ask is that you give me the courtesy of staying with me and completing the journey. I recall to my shame how, early in my "worship pilgrimage," I violently disagreed with authors and tossed their books aside, only to discover later that my immature fear was robbing me of the opportunity for growth. My personal "book burning" experiences said nothing about the books but a great deal about me!

When we get to the end of this book, it is not important that you and I agree on every jot and tittle. It is important that we both expand our vision of God, deepen our experience of worship, and broaden our love for God's people and our ministry to those who need Christ.

"God is trying to call us back to that for which He created us," wrote A. W. Tozer, "to worship Him and to enjoy Him forever!"[2]

Let's you and I heed that call together.

Now, let's begin.

FATHER,

Thank You for Your patience with me!

When I think of how many worship experiences I have wasted—and how many worship services I have criticized—I feel very ashamed.

Thank You for inviting me on this "worship pilgrimage," and for those who are going with me.

Guide us.

We have so much to learn!

More than anything else, we want to learn to worship You.

In the Name of Jesus, Your Son,

AMEN.

CHAPTER 2 *In which we attempt to define* worship

IF YOU AND I are to make any real progress in this pilgrimage, we must decide what we mean by *worship* and *transformation*. Let's begin with *worship* and then consider *transformation* in the next chapter.

I realize that definitions can *create* problems as well as *solve* them. The English novelist Samuel Butler wrote that a definition is "the enclosing of a wilderness of idea within a wall of words." My favorite example of that is Samuel Johnson's famous definition of *network:* "Any thing reticulated or decussated, at equal distances, with interstices between the intersections." Talk about wilderness!

THE PROBLEM OF DEFINITIONS

However, we must face the fact that some things are very difficult to define. A devoted husband and wife might have to struggle to define the love they feel so deeply, and a gifted artist may not be able to define "beauty." Even the great theologian St. Augustine had his troubles. "What, then, is time?" he asked. "If no one asks of me, I know; if I wish to explain to him who asks, I know not."

We must be careful, too, that our definition is not so high a wall that we find ourselves in an intellectical and emotional prison. Good definitions must set limits, but they must also leave room for expansion. It is all right to put up walls so long as you include a door and a few windows. This may have been what Erasmus meant when he wrote, "Every definition is dangerous."

We must also keep in mind that good definitions must relate to experience. They must not be merely intellectually constructed to satisfy the lexicographer! After all, the Bible does not give us many definitions, but it does major on demonstrations and descriptions. The

20

Bible is not a dictionary or an encyclopedia. Rather, it is a *Who's Who* of people who knew God, trusted Him, and got things accomplished. The cast of characters found in Scripture would agree with Thomas à Kempis: "I had rather feel compunction, than understand the definition thereof." Experience is important to understanding. ✳

As you probably know, our English word *worship* simply means "worth-ship." We worship that which is worthy. "You are worthy, O Lord, to receive glory and honor and power" (Rev. 4:11). "Worthy is the Lamb who was slain" (Rev. 5:12). Man is not worthy of worship, and certainly the idols that man makes are not worthy. Only God is worthy of our worship. What a person worships is a good indication of what is really valuable to him.

Four different Hebrew words are translated "worship" in the Authorized Version, but the one used most often is *shāchāh*, which means "to bow down, to do homage." It is first used in Genesis 18:2 where Abraham bowed down to the three visitors, one of whom (he discovered) was the Lord from heaven.

The key Greek word is *proskuneō*, which literally means "to kiss toward." It conveys the idea of showing reverence or doing obeisance, to God (John 4:21–24), man (Matt. 18:26), or even Satan (Rev. 13:4). Another important Greek word is *latreuō*, which basically means "to serve, minister" (see Matt. 4:10, Heb. 9:9 and 14, and Rev. 22:3 for examples). A related word is *leitourgos*, which means "a priestly minister" and gives us our English word *liturgy*. I will have more to say about this word when we consider the relationship between preaching and worship in a later chapter.

When you consider all of the words used for worship in both the Old and New Testaments, and when you put the meanings together, you find that worship involves both attitudes (awe, reverence, respect) and actions (bowing, praising, serving). It is both a subjective experience and an objective activity. Worship is not an unexpressed feeling, nor is it an empty formality. True worship is balanced and involves the mind, the emotions, and the will. It must be intelligent; it must reach deep within and be motivated by love; and it must lead to obedient actions that glorify God.

Evelyn Underhill has defined *worship* as "the total adoring response of man to the one Eternal God self-revealed in time."[3] I like that phrase "adoring response." It reminds me that worship is personal and passionate, not formal and cold; and that it is our response to the living God, voluntarily offered to Him as He has offered Himself to us.

In His conversation with the woman of Samaria, Jesus made it clear that there was both true worship and false worship, ignorant worship and intelligent worship (John 4:19-24). What passes for Christian worship, even in some of our churches, may not be acceptable to God at all. The Pharisees thought they were practicing exemplary worship, but Jesus thought otherwise: "These people draw near to Me with their mouth, and honor Me with their lips, but their heart is far from Me. And in vain they worship Me, teaching as doctrines the commandments of men" (Matt. 15:8, 9).

More about that later. What concerns us now is that we agree on the meaning of *worship*. One of my favorite definitions comes from William Temple, Archbishop of Canterbury (1942-44). I want to quote the entire paragraph from his *Readings in St. John's Gospel*, First Series.

> Both for perplexity and for dulled conscience the remedy is the same; sincere and spiritual worship. For worship is the submission of all our nature to God. It is the quickening of conscience by His holiness; the nourishment of mind with His truth; the purifying of imagination by His beauty; the opening of the heart to His love; the surrender of will to His purpose—and all of this gathered up in adoration, the most selfless emotion of which our nature is capable and therefore the chief remedy for that self-centeredness which is our original sin and the source of all actual sin. Yes—worship in spirit and truth is the way to the solution of perplexity and to the liberation from sin.[4]

To Temple, worship is the response of all that man is to all that God is and does. We do not worship God for what we get out of it, but because He is worthy of worship. "Whoever seeks God as a means toward desired ends will not find God," wrote A. W. Tozer. "God will not be used."[5] If you worship because it pays, it won't pay. Of course, this runs contrary to much of the popular preaching and teaching today that promises health, wealth, contentment, and a problem-free life to all who will "turn themselves over to God." Those who proclaim this pernicious doctrine would be brokenhearted if their own children loved them only for what they could get out of them.

Alfred North Whitehead could hardly be called an evangelical believer, yet he made a profound statement about worship that needs to be heeded today: "The worship of God is not a rule of safety—it is an adventure of the spirit, a flight after the unattainable."[6] "My soul thirsts for God, for the living God," wrote the psalmist. "When shall I come and appear before God?" (Ps. 42:2). Think of the dangerous experiences David went through in order to give us the psalms! Isaiah's vision of God's glorious throne eventually cost him his life, and Paul's experiences in the heavenlies brought him prison and death. True worship is not cheap entertainment.

Nor is it escape. I confess that I sometimes feel anguish within when I hear someone pray, "Oh Lord, thank You that we can come apart from the world to worship You, that we can leave our cares and burdens outside as we enter Your house." I may be wrong, but I carry my cares and burdens with me into the worship service, because it is there that I can get the right perspective to deal with them successfully. "When I thought how to understand this," Asaph wrote about his problem. "It was too painful for me—until I went into the sanctuary of God" (Ps. 73:16, 17). "He did not merely forget his problem for the time being," wrote D. Martyn Lloyd-Jones; "he found a solution."[7]

"God is our refuge *and strength* (Ps. 46:1, italics mine). God "hides" us so that He might help us. We are not refugees who are looking for escape; rather, we are wounded and weary soldiers who need rest and rehabilitation so we can go back into the battle. People who worship for "escape" do not know what true worship is, and they are wasting their time. True worship should lead to personal enrichment and enablement, the kind of spiritual strength that helps the believer carry the burdens and fight the battles of life.

Worship as escape becomes a selfish experience. Granted, all of us at one time or another have identified with David's groan, "Oh, that I had wings like a dove! I would fly away and be at rest" (Ps. 55:6). But I trust our identification with this selfish attitude has been only momentary, for if it becomes a settled way of life it leads to immaturity and unreality. It turns God into a celestial Physician Whose only task is to bind our wounds, and it robs us of the growth that can come when we discover the excitement of relating worship to daily life.

SUBJECTIVE AND OBJECTIVE ASPECTS

True worship has both its objective and subjective aspects, and we must maintain this balance. Jesus may have had this in mind when He said, "God is Spirit, and those who worship Him must worship in spirit and truth" (John 4:24). "In spirit" (note that the *s* is not capitalized) refers to the subjective side of worship; "in truth" refers to the objective side. If we do not submit to some kind of objective revelation, some Word from God, then our worship is ignorant and probably false. On the other hand, if we know the truth but merely go through the outward motions of worship, our worship will be hypocritical and empty. "When thou prayest," wrote John Bunyan, "rather let thy heart be without words, than thy words without heart." Paul called this formal worship "having a form of godliness but denying its power" (2 Tim. 3:5).

The important thing is that we keep the right balance. There is today such an emphasis on Bible knowledge that we are in danger of ignoring, or even opposing, personal spiritual experience. While we must not base our theology on experience, neither must we debase our theology by divorcing it from experience. If true worship is the response of the *whole* person to God, then we dare not neglect the emotions. We permit people to express their emotions at weddings, funerals, and athletic events, but not at a worship service. The important thing today seems to be that you mark your Bible and write outlines in your notebook, but whatever else you do, keep your emotions hidden!

This attitude, I am sure, is an overreaction to some of the extremes that Christians have seen in certain segments of the modern charismatic movement. While I personally deplore religious emotionalism, as opposed to true emotion, I must admit that I tend to agree with Bishop Handley Moule who said that he would rather tone down a fanatic than resurrect a corpse. It would be better not to have either extreme, of course; but if I have to make a choice, give me the fanatic.

The objective truth found in God's Word is important, but so is the subjective experience of that truth. In our quest to maintain our orthodoxy we have forgotten that the very word *orthodox* means "right praise" as well as "right opinion." We defend the faith and then descend into formalism, proud that our doctrine is correct but ignorant of the fact that our worship is dull and lifeless. Like the church at Laodicea, we are neither cold nor hot, but disgustingly lukewarm (Rev. 3:14–22). Campbell Morgan had this to say about the "formalists" in the church:

> He [Christ] does not ask that outward form be given up, or helpful rite abandoned. He will not suggest the setting aside of any form or ceremony that in itself is helpful. He has no criticism for these things. He permits the music and the methods, always providing that they are expressive of the deeper fact of life. These things He hates when they become the grave-clothes wrapped about death. The true ideal of worship is that of man communing with God.[8]

Once we understand the subjective and objective aspects of worship, we are better prepared to deal with some of the problems that worship seems to create. For one thing, we can better understand why different Christian communions express their worship in different ways. After all, if there is one God and one Bible, why should we not all worship in the same way? The answer is simply that we are all different and live in different cultural contexts.

Objective truth never changes, but our understanding of it deepens and our experience of it should become more and more meaningful. Divine revelation is one thing; human realization is something quite different. The Holy Spirit does not violate a believer's personality, but rather uses it to express praise to God. No two Christians have the identical worship experience even though they participate in the same service, at the same time, in the same sanctuary. For that matter, no two congregations, even in the same fellowship, express the same worship while following the same liturgy. Christian worship is both individual and corporate, personal and congregational. Led by the Spirit, we have the right, even the responsibility, to express our praise to God in the manner that best reflects our individual personalities and cultures. If all of us would keep this in mind, it might encourage a deeper appreciation for one another's form of worship.

THE ELEMENT OF MYSTERY

Before we try to tie all of this together, one more aspect of worship must be mentioned; and that is the fear of the Lord. If we major only on our "adoring response," we may find ourselves out of balance. After all, God's love for us is a *holy* love; and we must beware of trying to get chummy with God. I know, the apostle John leaned on the bosom of Jesus in the Upper Room; but he fell at the feet of Jesus when he beheld Him in His sovereign glory (Rev. 1:17). The old saints and mystics reveled in their experience of His love, but they also remembered that their God was "a consuming fire" (Heb. 12:29). As the Lord drew near to them, they kept in mind that He had not abdicated His throne but was still "high and lifted up." A. W. Tozer is right: "No one can know the true grace of God who has not first known the fear of God."[9]

Phillips Brooks once said that familiarity breeds contempt only with contemptible people or contemptible things. There is an undue familiarity with God that only proves that the worshiper does not really know God at all. True worship must always involve *mystery*. There are many things we cannot explain but that we can experience.

Mystery and humility go together, and there can be no real worship without humility. God reveals Himself but He rarely explains Himself. Christians do not live on explanations; they live on promises, and on deepening relationships. The unpardonable sin in the ministry today is for a man to admit, "I do not know"—but it should never be so. God deliberately keeps some things secret so that you and I will stay humble and learn to trust Him even when we do not understand what He is doing.

In our desire to explain everything and avoid whatever we cannot explain, we have almost robbed worship of the dimension of mystery. We no longer cry out with Paul, "Oh, the depth of the riches both of the wisdom and knowledge of God! How unsearchable are His judgments and His ways past finding out!" (Rom. 11:33). Paul prayed that we might "know the love of Christ which passes knowledge" (Eph. 3:19), a paradox indeed—a mystery if there ever was one.

"But you are promoting *mysticism!*" some orthodox saint may shout. "Mysticism is dangerous!" But that depends, my friend, on what kind of mysticism it is. A mystic is simply someone who believes that there is a real spiritual world behind the physical world that we see; and a Christian mystic sees Jesus Christ as Lord of both the seen and the unseen. Discussing what happened to the believers at Pentecost, Campbell Morgan wrote: "This is mysticism. Christianity is mysticism."[10]

Christian worship must be intelligent, but there are some things that we cannot explain. Christian worship must be based solidly on objective truth, but it must include subjective experience; and that is where Christian mysticism enters in. God is a Person, and our relationship to Him must be personal. Just as a devoted husband and wife, or parent and child, will experience what they cannot easily define or explain, so the devoted saint of God, thirsty for spiritual reality, will enjoy an experience of God that transcends the academic. Even the biblical writers had to resort to divinely inspired signs and symbols in order to express the inexpressible.

Certainly the spirits must be tried and experience tested by truth, or what we think is spiritual experience might turn out to be the flesh or the demonic. But the sincere Christian who knows his Bible and is yielded to the Spirit is not likely to be duped, especially if he keeps in touch with God's people in the church. The saints have a way of keeping us in balance.

A WORKING DEFINITION

No definition is final, so accept this one for the time being, and we can refine it as we go along:

Worship is the believer's response of all that he is—mind, emotions, will, and body—to all that God is and says and does. This response has its mystical side in subjective experience, and its practical side in objective obedience to God's revealed truth. It is a loving response that is balanced by the fear of the Lord, and it is a deepening response as the believer comes to know God better.

And what should be the result of all this? Transformation, which is the theme of our next chapter.

GRACIOUS FATHER,

Thank You for bringing us this far!
We still have a long way to go, but we feel You are with us and that You will teach us.
Deliver us from getting out of balance and divorcing our brains from our hearts.
We do want our worship to be intelligent, but we also want it to be fervent.
May head and heart be united by Your Spirit.
May our "adoring response" bring joy to Your heart!
In the Savior's Name,
AMEN.

CHAPTER 3 *In which we discuss transformation and discover how dangerous it can be*

WE WORSHIP GOD because He is worthy and not because we as worshipers get something out of it. If we look upon worship only as a means of getting something from God, rather than giving something to God, then we make God our servant instead of our Lord, and the elements of worship become a cheap formula for selfish gratification. We then become like those backslidden priests that the prophet Malachi denounced, men who said, "It is useless to serve God; what profit is it that we have kept His ordinance, and that we have walked as mourners before the LORD of hosts?" (Mal. 3:14).

Worshiping God with a wrong motive can be as deadening as worshiping the wrong God with a sincere motive. Both are wrong, but certainly the enlightened Christian faces a greater judgment than the sincere pagan. After all, we *know* the God we worship! We live in His world; we bear His image; and as believers, we even belong to His family. We have His revelation in His Word and the personal instruction of His Spirit. The believer who has a pragmatic approach to worship has certainly forgotten all of this and has turned God into a celestial Servant Who rewards him for his faithful worship.

We worship God because He is worthy and because He has commanded us to worship Him. However, this is not to say that there are no personal benefits from worshiping God, because there are. God has ordained that everything we *are* and *do* shall flow out of worship as "blessed by-products" of our fellowship with God. True spiritual worship ought to contribute something powerful and lasting to our personalities, our relationships, our service, and our total lives as Christians.

According to Albert W. Palmer, worship "means a release of energy. It puts into life something which steps it up to a higher voltage.

29

Through worship man comes to God at first hand, has an immediate experience with God, and goes forth transformed and stimulated to new levels of endeavor."[11]

Transformed. That is the word we are interested in. If true worship is anything, it is a transforming experience. We need to understand this word and then discover what kind of transformation takes place in the life of the person who worships God "in spirit and truth."

METAMORPHOSIS VS. MASQUERADE

When I was a lad in grade school, our class spent several weeks watching a cocoon and hoping that a beautiful butterfly would emerge. We were studying metamorphosis, that marvelous process of nature that changes tadpoles into frogs and caterpillars into moths or butterflies. Little did I know that one day I would meet that word *metamorphosis* in a seminary Greek class.

The Greek word *metamorphoumai* (the passive form of *metamorphoō*) means "to be changed into another form," but this change *comes from within*. In other words, the change on the outside is the normal and natural expression of the nature on the inside. You would never produce a butterfly by pinning wings on a worm! The changes must come from within.

There is another Greek word that describes changes on the outside that do *not* come from within. It is *metaschēmatizomai* and it is usually translated "fashioned" or "conformed." (A related word is *suschēmatizomai*.) When a Christian conforms to this world and fashions his life after the pattern of unbelievers, he is changing the outside, *but the change is not coming from the inside*. It is not metamorphosis; it is *masquerade*.

There is a striking illustration of this difference given by Paul in 2 Corinthians 11:13—"For such are false apostles, deceitful workers, transforming themselves into apostles of Christ." These false teachers adopted the disguise of true apostles of Christ, but in reality they were the ministers of Satan. Their outward change was a masquerade, not a metamorphosis. The outward image did not agree with the inward nature. They were only pretending.

Our Lord's transfiguration illustrates the meaning of *metamorphoumai*: "and He was transfigured before them. His face shone like the sun, and His clothes became as white as the light" (Matt. 17:2). What did the disciples see? The glory of God that was within Him, radiating in shadowless splendor! The apostle John wrote: "And we beheld His glory, the glory as of the only begotten of the Father, full of grace and truth" (John 1:14). And Peter testified, "We . . . were eyewitnesses of His majesty" (2 Pet. 1:16).

Our Lord's transfiguration was not a masquerade. The angels did not shine spotlights on Him: The glory came from within. He was transformed on the outside by revealing the glory that was on the inside.

It is this kind of experience to which you and I are called by God. He wants to transform us. He also wants to work through us to transform the people and circumstances that make up our lives. Every Christian is either a "conformer" or a "transformer." We are either fashioning our lives by pressure from without, or we are transforming our lives by power from within. The difference is—worship.

LIVING AS A SACRIFICE

Now we are ready to consider the two texts I quoted in chapter 1—Romans 12:1, 2 and 2 Corinthians 3:18—because both of them explain what this spiritual metamorphosis is and how we can begin to experience it.

> I beseech you therefore, brethren, by the mercies of God, that you present your bodies a living sacrifice, holy, acceptable to God, which is your reasonable service [spiritual worship]. And do not be conformed to this world, but be transformed [*metamorphoumai*] by the renewing of your mind, that you may prove what is that good and acceptable and perfect will of God.

Paul is contrasting two ways of life, that of the believer who is being transformed by God, and that of the believer who is being conformed to the world. It is the contrast between metamorphosis and masquerade. As I said earlier, the "transformer" lives by power from within, but the "conformer" lives by pressure from without. The paraphrase by J. B. Phillips brings this out beautifully: "Don't let the world around you squeeze you into its own mould, but let God remake you so that your whole attitude of mind is changed."

The image here is that of the priest offering a sacrifice on the altar. The Greek word translated "present" is the technical term for the offering of a sacrifice. The difference, of course, is that you and I are to be *living* sacrifices and not corpses. We are to be like Jesus Christ Who today bears on His body the marks of Calvary. He is a living sacrifice.

While I want to avoid formulas that smack of technique, I cannot help but see in this text three gifts that God wants me to present to Him in order that I may worship Him and experience His transforming powers.

To begin with, *God wants my body*. The Greek verb indicates that this is to be a once-for-all presentation, as I give my body to God to be used for His service. However, this does not prevent me from reaffirming this dedication daily when I set aside time to worship the Lord. Israel had its "continual burnt offering," morning and evening (Exod. 29:38–42), and this may be a good pattern for us to follow today.

It is unfortunate that an overdose of the wrong kind of Greek philosophy has infected Christian theology and given people the idea that the body is sinful. Or that worship is an experience so "spiritual" that it denies the body or the use of anything material. The human body is neutral; it can be an instrument of sin or of holiness. "And do not present your members as instruments of unrighteousness to sin," Paul admonished the Romans, "but present yourselves to God as being alive from the dead [living sacrifices!], and your members as instruments of righteousness to God" (Rom. 6:13).

The body of the Christian is God's temple (1 Cor. 6:19, 20) and God's tool (Rom. 6:13). God lives in the believer's body! God can use that body to accomplish His work and glorify His name. Paul prayed that Christ might be magnified in his body (Phil. 1:20). "Let your light so shine before men, that they may see your good works and glorify your Father in heaven" (Matt. 5:16). Worship must not stop with a personal mystical experience. It must lead to a practical ministry experience, something we do with our bodies, that brings help to others and honor to God. "The best public worship," wrote Bishop J. C. Ryle, "is that which produces the best private Christianity."[12]

The second gift God asks for is *my mind*. Since we are made in the image of God, we have intelligence, emotion, and will. To be sure, all three suffer from the terrible effects of man's fall; but God can renew them and use them for His glory. A balanced Christian life involves more than duty (the will) and delight (the emotions); it also involves discernment (the mind). Passionate action without intelligence is fanaticism. We are to love God with the mind as well as the heart (Luke 10:27).

Christians should think the way God thinks and not the way the world thinks. The believer's mind ought to be so saturated with divine truth that it can determine the divine perspective on every question, issue, or decision. A renewed mind is a mind alert to the world's false philosophies and Satan's subtle strategy. A renewed mind directs the believer to offer intelligent worship to the Lord. "All Christian worship," says Dr. John Stott, "public and private, should be an intelligent response to God's self-revelation in his words and works recorded in Scripture."[13]

It is the Word of God, taught by the Spirit of God, that renews the mind. This Word may come through preaching and teaching, through personal witness in word or song, or through study and meditation; but it always comes (if we are receptive) with that power to renew us. This is why the believer must spend time daily with the Bible, reading and meditating; and why the Word must be an important part of public worship.

God asks for my body, my mind, and *my will*. For the most part, my mind controls my body, and my will controls my mind. I usually think about what I *want* to think about. Christianity is basically a religion centering on man's will, not man's feelings. Christian love is not a feeling; it is an act of the will. Otherwise, Jesus could not *command* us to love one another. I am not denying that there is a wonderful emotional dimension to Christian love; I am only emphasizing that Christian love is primarily what we *do*, not what we *feel*. This makes the will very important in Christian living.

Three times our Lord prayed in Gethsemane, "O My Father, if it is possible, let this cup pass from me; nevertheless, not as I will, but as You will" (Matt. 26:39).

God does not have three wills—one good, another acceptable, and yet another perfect—because a perfect God can only will for us that which is perfect. The will of God is not like the merchandise in a mail-order catalog, labeled "Good," "Better," and "Best" and if you want "Best," you have to pay more for it. God has one will for your life; anything else is simply not what He willed, even though He may permit it. We prove *by experience* (that is the meaning of the Greek verb) that God's will is good, pleasing to Him, and complete in every aspect. We want nothing more, nothing less, nothing else.

God expects body, mind, and will to be yielded to Him and to be used by the Spirit as we worship Him. He also wants us to worship Him in love from a heart that is caught up in Him and His beauty. But more about this later. We must now turn to the second key "transformation" text, 2 Corinthians 3:18.

RADIATING THE GLORY OF GOD

Before we examine the text, we must understand some of the background of this chapter. Paul is contrasting the ministry of grace with the ministry of law under the old covenant. The law of Moses was written on stones, but God's Word in the new covenant is written on the human heart by the Spirit of God. It is a ministry of internal change, not external compulsion. Furthermore, the old covenant was a ministry of death; but the new covenant ministry of grace brings life. Under law, the people were in bondage; but under grace, they enjoy spiritual liberty.

But Paul's greatest emphasis is on the contrast between the glory of the old covenant and the glory of the new covenant. There certainly was glory under the Law: God revealed His glory at Mount Sinai, and then His glory dwelt in the holy of holies in the tabernacle. When Moses worshiped God on the top of the mount, he picked up some of that glory so that his face shone when he returned to the camp (see Exod. 34:29–35). Moses was not *radiating* glory from within; he was only *reflecting* glory that had been seen on the mount.

And that glory faded away! It was temporary. Moses had to put a veil over his face so that the people could not see the fading glory (2 Cor. 3:13). The glory of the law was temporary, but the glory of the new covenant is both permanent and increasing. It is getting more and more glorious! Instead of veiling our faces, we want the world to see what the grace of God can do in the life of the Christian. We have nothing to hide!

But we all, with unveiled face, beholding as in a mirror the glory of the Lord, are being transformed [*metamorphoumai*] into the same image from glory to glory, just as by the Spirit of the Lord. (2 Cor. 3:18)

The mirror is a symbol of God's Word (James 1:23–25) in which we see God's Son. As we worship Him and behold His glory, we are transformed by His Spirit to share in His own image and glory. Instead of hiding a fading glory, we reveal an increasing glory that causes others to see Christ and honor Him. "But the path of the just is like the shining sun, that shines ever brighter unto the perfect day" (Prov. 4:18).

We become like the god that we worship (Ps. 115:8). As we worship the true God, in spirit and truth, we are transformed to become more like Him. What we are and what we do are both determined by what we worship.

Paul's instruction in Romans 12:1, 2 involves a crisis, but 2 Corinthians 3:18 speaks about a process. The two go together; for as we yield body, mind, and will to the Lord, and as we meditate on His Word, the Spirit of God transforms us into "living sacrifices" who have "renewed minds," people who radiate the glory of God. We become transformers, not conformers.

However, a warning is needed here: we must not put the emphasis on our own spiritual condition but on the glory of God. There are "religious hypochondriacs" who are so wrapped up in the techniques of spiritual living that they become unbalanced and unspiritual. "Those Christians whose chief concern is their own spiritual condition," wrote Washington Gladden, "are a very poor sort of Christians. A self-conscious holiness is a contradiction in terms."[14] These people perform so many spiritual dissections that they have no strength left to serve the Lord! And they get so concerned about themselves that they neglect ministering to their fellow Christians. It is a false holiness that reveals none of the glory of God.

A CALL TO TRANSFORMATION

What we have been discussing seems to be very exciting: beholding God's glory in the Word, seeing God's Son in the Word, being transformed by the Spirit, radiating God's glory in our daily lives, and becoming more like Jesus Christ. Why would any Christian believer not want this kind of worship experience?

For one thing, this kind of experience demands devotion and discipline, and many believers are not interested in discipline. Paul admonished young Timothy to exercise himself to godliness (1Tim. 4:7, 8), suggesting that the believer needs the same kind of discipline that makes an athlete successful. If each of us devoted himself or herself to spiritual things with the same kind of intensity and discipline that the Olympic contender shows, we would be much better Christians than we now are!

But there is another reason why some believers steer away from this kind of worship experience: the consequences may be dangerous. Each of us must honestly answer the question, "Am I willing to pay the price, in my own home and church, so that I might have a worship experience that will please God and accomplish His purposes in my life?" It is not likely that many of us will become martyrs, but we may find ourselves suffering in other ways. It is my feeling that many Christians do not want a transforming experience of worship. So, when a transformed believer shows up among them, they are immediately threatened by his presence—and this can lead to some difficult situations in homes and churches. *"Transformers" do not create problems; they reveal them.*

Transformers are participants, but most Christians want to be spectators. Most Christians are content to attend church, give their money, and allow a professional staff to "lead in worship" and provide religious entertainment Sunday by Sunday.

Transformers patiently wait for the Spirit to change them and make them more like the Savior, but most church members want immediate results that can be categorized and computed. The transformer looks for *fruit* while the conformer calculates *results*.

Transformers quietly resist the "celebrityism" that marks the church today, while many professed believers are so taken up with "famous Christians" that their dedication to them almost becomes cultic. A believer with a renewed mind is happy to hear God's Word from any sincere servant of God, known or unknown; but other Christians insist on listening to the "leading expositors of the day," who are often media superstars.

Transformers trust God to work as they worship, pray and sow the seed of the Word, but conformers run from seminar to seminar, seeking to discover new techniques for getting God's work done in this world. They often follow the latest fads without asking where these fads originated or on what biblical principles they are founded.

Transformers have a different set of values from that of their conforming friends. They are not impressed by budgets and buildings, but they do look for fruit that glorifies God. To them, it is more important to care for the needy than to build another building or start a new "ministry" that is really not needed. Transformers would rather see a growing fellowship divide and start a new church where one is needed than unite to build a larger sanctuary.

Transformers are not concerned about getting the approval of the world or being popular with the world's leaders. They are content to live to please the Lord and serve others. If they are noticed, they get embarrassed; if they are unnoticed, they rejoice. So-called Christian celebrities do not interest them, particularly those of the "Hollywood" variety who sing in nightclubs on Saturday night and then in a church service on Sunday morning.

Now you understand why I warned you: if you decide you want to pursue a meaningful worship experience, *do not expect the encouragement*. True worship examines us deeply; our motives and our values are scrutinized by God. In worship, God is calling us to wholeness; but first He must reveal our brokenness and our blemishes. He is calling us to spiritual health, but first He must expose our "wounds and bruises and putrefying sores" (Isa. 1:6); and we cannot ask for a second opinion.

In short, the most dangerous thing we can do is to return to spiritual worship. It would mean the end of the personality cults that have invaded the church. It would also mean the end of the "Christian consumerism" that has so twisted our sense of spiritual values. I have no doubt that the church that returned to true worship would lose people—"important" people—and probably have to make drastic cuts in the budget.

But then—*something would happen!*

A beautiful new sense of spiritual reality would result, with people glorifying God instead of praising men. There would be a new unity among God's people, no matter what label they might wear; and the divisive spirit of competition would gradually vanish. Nobody would be going around asking, "Who is the greatest in the kingdom of heaven?"

Some organizations and "ministries" would go out of business and new ministries would appear. Congregations would start to make better use of their facilities, and money that would have been spent on brick and mortar would be invested in serving people in the name of Jesus. Small, struggling churches would merge and assist each other, and the watching world would see new demonstrations of love and harmony.

There would be new power in prayer and worship and a new attention to the Word. Families would pray together and do so joyfully. Marriages would be mended. Satan would be defeated in his attempts to destroy God's people and God's church.

This is not to suggest that all our problems would be solved and the kingdom would be established. No, we would face a whole new set of problems; but they would be caused by the expansion of spiritual ministry and not the expression of carnal Christians. Most of the problems in the church today are not caused by spiritual growth and development. They are caused by carnal, worldly people—including church leaders—who stand in the way of spiritual growth. Ministers and church officers must spend so much time running around to put out brush fires that they have no time left for the work of the ministry itself.

And we have accepted this sick situation as normal!

Why? Because we have so long been away from the bright light of true worship that we can no longer see clearly to evaluate our own situation. Our measurements for ministry and for spiritual success are so unbiblical that we are leading one another astray and not knowing it. We are like the pilot who announced from the cockpit, "Folks, we are lost, but we are making very good time!"

The goal of worship is Christlikeness in our character and conduct. The more we become like Christ, the more we will be treated by others the way He was treated:

They crucified Him because He said He would put an end to the building program and tear down the temple.

They crucified Him because He opposed the religious merchandising that was going on in the temple.

Then they stoned Stephen—another man with a shining face—

because he dared to say that God did not live in the temple but would one day destroy it.

God's call to true worship, to an experience of transformation, is a call to dangerous and costly Christian living.

It is a call to wonder, to witness, and to warfare.

Will you heed the call?

GRACIOUS FATHER,

We did not realize when we started this journey that there would be a price to pay.

We confess that we are comfortable as conformers.

We are not sure we really want to be transformers!

Father, do a beautiful work in our lives so that others will want this same work in their lives.

Give us patience. Give us humility. Keep us from judging others in our fellowship.

Remind us that You look with favor on those who are poor, and of a contrite spirit, who tremble at Your word (Isa. 66:2).

Father, we are about to consider the wonder of worship. Our minds and hearts are so jaded by a multitude of shallow, counterfeit experiences, that we have lost that thrilling sense of wonder.

Restore to us, O God, the wonder of it all!

In the Name of Him Whose Name is Wonderful,
AMEN.

PART II

Worship Involves Wonder

Let others wrangle, I will wonder.
ST. AUGUSTINE

When wonder is dead, the soul becomes a dry bone.
BISHOP WILLIAM QUAYLE[15]

CHAPTER 4 *In which we get involved in the wonder of wonder*

TRUE WORSHIP INVOLVES wonder, witness, and warfare; but we have to start with wonder. "Wonder is the basis of worship," wrote Thomas Carlyle;[16] and Emerson said that wonder was "the seed of science."[17] "Philosophy begins in wonder," said Alfred North Whitehead;[18] so it appears that wonder is a priceless ingredient in the life of any thinking person.

The trouble is that wonder is a *rare* ingredient. You do not often find it present in most modern worship. After all, what is there to wonder about? Why should there be any mystery in the worship experience of the average congregation? We *know* all about God, because we know our Bibles so well. We study; we listen to sermons, in person and by means of cassettes; we read books that explain what God and the Christian life are all about. We have outlined the Bible, analyzed God's attributes, and charted the ages. What is there to elicit our wonder?

Furthermore, we live in the space age and have watched rockets and space shuttles take off and return. We have witnessed man walking on the moon. Thanks to TV documentaries, we have seen everything from the conception of a baby to the eruption of a volcano. We have watched flowers grow, fish spawn, and stars become supernovas. There is no more mystery, no more wonder in our world.

"The world will never starve for want of wonders," wrote Gilbert Keith Chesterton, "but only for want of wonder."

The church today is imperiled by what it *thinks* it understands. Most preaching focuses on *explaining* something and neglects to admit the things that cannot be explained. "We are dwellers in the regions of explanation," wrote Bishop William Quayle back in 1910. He should see the situation today! We are no longer struck by the wonder and mystery of God and His revelation of grace. We have descriptions and definitions for everything theological, as well as approved pigeonholes assigned for each item.

This is not to suggest that we put our minds in neutral when we participate in Christian worship! But it does mean that we learn to accept things we cannot understand, and appreciate things that we can admire but not explain. A leading modern theologian, T. F. Torrance, states it perfectly: "Worship is the exercise of the mind in the contemplation of God in which wonder and awe play an important part in stretching and enlarging our vision, or in opening up our conceptual forms to take in that which by its nature far outruns them."[19]

Perhaps this is one lesson Jesus had in mind when He told His disciples to become as little children. A child's life is filled with wonder, and this sense of wonder enables him or her to see things in life that escape the rest of us. My grandchildren can squat and stare at a flower or an insect with an imaginative interest that I hope will never be lost. Alas, tests show that a child's creativity—which includes imagination and wonder—diminishes by 90 percent between ages five and seven! When an adult gets to be forty, he has about 2 percent of the creativity he had when he was five years old. No wonder the children sang to Jesus in the temple while the theologically trained adults tried to silence them. "There are children playing in the street," said J. Robert Oppenheimer, "who could solve some of my top problems in physics," because they have modes of sensory perception that I lost long ago."[20]

WHAT IS WONDER?

Many different words cluster around the idea of wonder: *amazement, surprise, astonishment, bewilderment, admiration, awe,* and *fascination,* to name but a few. The word in the Hebrew Bible ("His name shall be called Wonderful . . ." Isa. 9:6) means "to distinguish, to separate." It carries the idea of that which is unique, distinguished by difference. In our English versions, the word is translated "hidden, marvelous, too high, too hard (difficult), etc." The Greek words in the New Testament are similar: "amazement, marvelous, admiration, wonderful work, something strange."

In spite of all these synonyms, we must recognize the fact that true wonder is not a passing emotion or some kind of shallow excitement. It has depth to it. True wonder reaches right into your heart and mind and shakes you up. It not only has depth, it has value; it enriches your life. Wonder is not cheap amusement that brings a smile to your face. It is an encounter with reality—with God—that brings awe to your heart. You are overwhelmed with an emotion that is a mixture of gratitude, adoration, reverence, fear—and love. You are not looking for explanations; you are lost in the wonder of God.

Some people have the idea that wonder is born of ignorance. The unlearned savage is frightened, then fascinated, by the shortwave radio or the jet plane, while the educated tourist takes both for granted. But wonder is not born of ignorance: it is born of knowledge. The more a truly reverent person knows about a flower or an insect or God, the more overwhelmed he is. Scientific or theological *facts* may give some people a big head, but *truths* give to the reverent saint a burning heart, a thrilling encounter with God.

This is the paradox of Christian worship: we seek to see the invisible, know the unknowable, comprehend the incomprehensible, and experience the eternal. Like David, we thirst after God and we are both satisfied and dissatisfied. Like Moses, we cry out for His glory, all the while knowing that our mortal eyes could never behold God's glory in its fullness. Like Peter, we wrestle with a tension within: we want to follow Him, and yet we cry out, "Depart from me, for I am a sinful man!"

"The fairest thing we can experience is the mysterious," wrote Albert Einstein in *The World as I See It*. "He who knows it not, can no longer wonder, no longer feel amazement, is as good as dead, a snuffed-out candle."

Emerson was right: wonder is "the seed of science." It is also the seed of spiritual knowledge and understanding. "To be surprised, to wonder, is to begin to understand," wrote José Ortega y Gasset. Moses staring at the burning bush and Peter struggling with the breaking nets illustrate this truth clearly. Both men had their lives changed because they were amazed at something God did in their lives.

Where has our God-given sense of wonder gone? It began to leave us when we started to learn about our scientific world where there is a recipe for everything. God was replaced by a formula. Success is guaranteed if you only follow the correct steps. There is an explanation for everything.

This is, of course, a false "scientific approach," because true science thrives on wonder. However, this approach has invaded the church and we are now the victims of definitions, analyses, outlines, charts, and formulas. The church used to live on the dangerous but exciting edge of miracle; but today the church has both feet planted firmly on the ground and does not dare to venture out where the bushes are burning.

A RETURN TO WONDER

Certainly I am not suggesting that the church jettison twenty centuries of theological achievement. If anything, we need to dig again the old wells and drink from them; but we must not filter the living water through our bland systems and rob it of its power. We need a return to wonder. We need a new emphasis on the mystery of things. For all of his great theological brilliance, the apostle Paul never lost his sense of the wonder and mystery of the faith. "Oh, the depth of the riches both of the wisdom and knowledge of God!" he exclaimed. "How unsearchable are His judgments and His ways past finding out!" (Rom. 11:33). And Paul wrote that after he had penned three profound chapters on the sovereignty of God. When our theologians learn to move as Paul did from theology to doxology, we will have taken a giant step toward the recovering of mystery and wonder in worship.

In fact, the place to begin is with *the wonder of wonder itself*. What a thrilling thing it is that you and I, made in the image of God, can participate in wonder! As long as we maintain that childlike spirit, that attitude of humility that says "Why have you chosen me, Lord?"—then we can grow in our sense of wonder. The world both without and within becomes aglow with the excitement of the wonder of it all. "What is man that You are mindful of him, and the son of man that You visit him?" (Ps. 8:4).

One of the sayings attributed to Jesus, not written in Scripture but found in the *Gospel According to the Hebrews*, is: "He that has marvelled shall reign, and he that has reigned shall rest."[21] The statement may not be from the lips of Jesus, but the sentiment is certainly

Christian. The believer who lives without wonder is a slave, not a king, and the world is a frightening place to him. But the believer who sees wonder in himself, in others, in creation, in the church, in God, actually lives like a king and transforms whatever he experiences because he himself is being transformed. Even that spiritual transformation is a part of the wonder of it all!

When we are in our private devotions, our daily work, or the corporate worship of the church, we must cultivate this attitude of wonder. We can never tell when we may encounter our own burning bush or breaking net.

And that encounter could mark the beginning of the transformation of your life and your church.

LOVING FATHER,

Make my heart like that of a child.
Give me again the excitement and joy of wonder.
  How wonderful it is that I am even able to wonder!
Remove the scales from my eyes,
  the callousness from my heart,
  the stubbornness from my will,
  and enable me to enjoy the wonder of it all.
Deliver me from routine worship,
  from "business as usual,"
  from form without force and liturgy without life.
May Your Holy Spirit energize that "new creation"
  that is now within me,
  and may it be ever new, ever wonderful,
  to the glory of Your Name.
AMEN.

CHAPTER 5 *In which we cautiously attempt to discuss the wonder of God*

DURING A MONDAY-NIGHT prayer meeting at Spurgeon's Pastors' College, one of the men stood and prayed, "O Thou that art encinctured with an auriferous zodiac!"[22]

Contrast that artificial expression (based on Rev. 1:13) with this burst of praise from St. Augustine:

> Most high, most excellent, most potent, most omnipotent; most piteous and most just; most hidden and most near; most beauteous and most strong, stable, yet contained of none; unchangeable, yet changing all things; never new, never old; making all things new, yet bringing old age upon the proud and they know it not; always working, yet ever at rest; gathering, yet needing nothing; sustaining, pervading, and protecting; creating, nourishing, and developing; seeking, and yet possessing all things.[23]

(If you skipped that last paragraph, or just skimmed over it, please go back and read it meditatively. Thanks!)

The difference, of course, is that the young student wanted to *impress* his friends while Augustine wanted to *express* his sincere praise to God. The difference between impressing and expressing is fundamental to our worship of God. "But all their works they do to be seen by men," said Jesus in His indictment of the Pharisees (Matt. 23:5), an indictment that we do well to heed today.

God is wonderful in what He is, what He says, and what He does; and this wonder is beyond us. "Behold, God is great, and we do not know him," said Elihu (Job 36:26). "Can you search out the deep things of God?" asked Zophar of Job. "Can you find out the limits of the Almighty?" (Job 11:7). And we recall again Paul's cry: "Oh, the depth of the riches both of the wisdom and knowledge of God! How unsearchable are His judgments and His ways past finding out!" (Rom. 11:33).

Our problem, of course, is that we are finite humans seeking to understand an infinite God and then to express to Him our praise in words that are severely limited. Whether we like it or not, we must struggle with human feelings and words as we feebly attempt to express what is inexpressible. As Evelyn Underhill states it, we must "adapt the machinery and language of human emotion";[24] otherwise, we are left speechless. While there certainly is a place in Christian worship for the silence of meditation and contemplation, a worship perhaps too deep for words, the saints of God both in Scripture and in history usually gave expression to their praise, in human words and human terms.

The Incarnation gives us the freedom to do this: God Himself came in human form and expressed divine thoughts in human language. The wonder of God is revealed to us in words that are wrapped around images, symbols, types, pictures. We can never enter into the wonder of God simply by intelligence and understanding alone; we must also exercise our imagination. We must attempt, with the aid of the Spirit of God, to grasp some of the wonder of God as it is presented to us in Scripture.

The danger here is that the imagination may run away with us, and we might start turning spiritual vision into human fantasy. In one of her letters to Thomas Higginson, the poetess Emily Dickenson thus described her family: "They are religious, except me, and address an eclipse every morning, whom they call their 'Father.'"[25] I wonder how many worshipers today have such a nebulous imaginative view of God.

"They [humans] have never known that ghastly luminosity, that stabbing and searing glare which makes the background of permanent pain to our lives," the demon Screwtape writes to his nephew in C. S. Lewis's *The Screwtape Letters*. "If you look into your patient's mind when he is praying, you will not find *that*. If you examine the object to which he is attending, you will find that it is a composite object containing many quite ridiculous ingredients. . . . But whatever the nature of the composite object, you must keep him praying to *it*—to the thing that he has made, not to the Person who has made him."[26]

Unless imagination is made captive to the truth of God's Word, it will lead us astray. How easy it is for the imaginative to become the imaginary. Joseph Joubert was right: "He who has imagination without learning has wings and no feet."[27] Unworthy *mental* images of God are just as idolatrous as images made of wood or stone. "Spiritual exercises" that encourage the worshiper to imagine the Savior in some biblical scene, and from this picture produce "devotional feelings," are dangerous and unbiblical. The feelings may be as imaginary as the picture. For that matter, we might end up worshiping our feelings instead of worshiping God.

THE WONDER OF THE CREATOR

The wonder of God is revealed in one way or another throughout the entire Bible, but I want to focus on four of the worship hymns recorded in the book of Revelation. What the hosts of heaven are saying and doing in their worship ought to be worthy of our study and imitation.

The first hymn is found in Revelation 4 where the emphasis is on the wonder of God as Creator. Let's read through this fascinating chapter:

> After these things I looked, and behold, a door standing open in heaven. And the first voice which I heard was like a trumpet speaking with me, saying, "Come up here, and I will show you things which must take place after this."
>
> Immediately I was in the Spirit; and behold, a throne set in heaven, and One sat on the throne. And He who sat there was like a jasper and a sardius stone in appearance; and there was a rainbow around the throne, in appearance like an emerald. Around the throne were twenty-four thrones, and on the thrones I saw twenty-four elders sitting, clothed in white robes; and they had crowns of gold on their heads. And from the throne proceeded lightnings, thunderings and voices. Seven lamps of fire were burning before the throne, which are the seven Spirits of God.
>
> Before the throne there was a sea of glass, like crystal. And in the midst of the throne, and around the throne, were four living creatures full of eyes in front and in back. The first living creature was like a lion, the second living creature like a calf, the third living creature had a face like a man, and the fourth living creature was like a flying eagle. The four living creatures, each having six wings, were full of eyes around and within. And they do not rest day or night, saying:

"Holy, Holy, holy,
   Lord God Almighty,
   Who was and is and is to come!"

Whenever the living creatures give glory and honor and thanks to Him who sits on the throne, who lives forever and ever, the twenty-four elders fall down before Him who sits on the throne and worship Him who lives forever and ever, and cast their crowns before the throne, saying:

"You are worthy, O Lord,
   To receive glory and honor and power;
   For You created all things,
   And by Your will they exist and were created."

If, as you read the passage, you had a feeling that it was very familiar, perhaps it is because Revelation 4 is the basis for Reginald Heber's popular hymn, "Holy, Holy, Holy." You noted, of course, that the theme of their worship is God the Creator.

"If the stars should appear one night in a thousand years," wrote Ralph Waldo Emerson, "how would men believe and adore, and preserve for many generations the remembrance of the city of God which had been shown."[28] David expressed the same sentiment centuries ago: "The heavens declare the glory of God; and the firmament shows His handiwork" (Ps. 19:1).

What we see in creation pretty much depends on what we have in our hearts. The adoring believer joyfully accepts the creation as a window through which the Creator may be seen. The covetous unbeliever looks at creation and sees, not a window, but a mirror. (The covetous *believer* could make the same mistake.) When we look at creation and see only ourselves, then we start to think that *we* are the Creator; and the result is idolatry.

For since the creation of the world His invisible attributes are clearly seen, being understood by the things that are made, even His eternal power and Godhead; so that they are without excuse, because, although they knew God, they did not glorify Him as God, nor were thankful, but became futile in their thoughts, and their foolish hearts were darkened . . . who exchanged the truth of God for the lie, and worshiped and served the creature rather than the Creator, who is blessed forever. Amen. (Rom. 1:20, 21, 25)

When we want to enjoy creation *without honoring the Creator*, we end up exploiting creation just to satisfy our selfish appetites. We become covetous and idolatrous, and this is the root cause of the ecological problems the world faces today. When we start to "play God," we end up destroying what God has given us "richly . . . to enjoy" (1 Tim. 6:17).

As you listen to the "creation hymn" recorded in Revelation 4, and as you witness the scene described, you discover a great deal about God. He is certainly the *sovereign* God, for He is enthroned (the word *throne* is used fourteen times in this chapter) and His name is "Lord God Almighty." In the Greek text, this name is used six times in Revelation, and "Almighty" is used nine times. The only other book in the Bible that uses this name as extensively is the book of Job, where God is certainly seen in His sovereignty and power.

The heavenly hosts worship a sovereign God Who is *holy*. The word means "separate, set apart, unique." There is none like Him. He is pure: "God is light" (1 John 1:5). This means that creation is not sinful, for a holy God would not create sinful matter. Creation is God's holy gift to us and, as stewards, we must use this gift for the good of man and the glory of God.

This holy sovereign God is *eternal:* "who was and is and is to come" (v. 8). Matter is not eternal, but God is; therefore we do not worship creation but the Creator. To put material things ahead of God is idolatry.

The living creatures that John describes are similar to the creatures that Ezekiel saw and called *cherubim* (Ezek. 1; 10). The four "faces" of the creatures remind me of God's covenant with Noah after the Flood (Gen. 9:8–17). God promised to protect all creation from another flood, and He gave the rainbow as the sign of the covenant (note the rainbow around God's throne, Rev. 4:3). The covenant was made with man, the birds, the cattle and the beasts of the field—the very "faces" displayed by the heavenly creatures. It seems that these "living creatures" symbolize God's covenant with creation and God's care of creation. He is the *faithful* God who keeps His covenant and watches over His creation.

If the twenty-four elders symbolize God's covenant people—twelve tribes of Israel plus the twelve apostles—then we have the glorified saints in heaven falling down at God's throne and worshiping the Creator. In Revelation 5 you will find this same group worshiping the Redeemer, but the book begins with their worship of the Creator. Why? Because until man admits he is a creature who is answerable to a Creator, he can never confess that he is a sinner who needs a Redeemer. This explains why Paul, when addressing Gentile audiences, began with God the Creator (Acts 14:5–17 and 22–31). To the Jews, Paul's emphasis was on God's covenant with Israel; to the Gentiles, his emphasis was God's covenant with creation. We need this same emphasis today both in our witness and our worship.

In my early years as a Christian, I was often upset when I attended a service where "creation hymns" were sung. "The important thing is the cross!" I would argue. "Let the liberals sing about the birds and flowers!" How wrong I was! I did not realize then as I do now that the God of creation and the God of salvation are the same God, and that these must not be divorced from each other.

A beautiful hymn by John Austin says it perfectly.

> Hark, my soul, how everything
> Strives to serve our bounteous King;
> Each a double tribute pays,
> Sings its part, and then obeys.
>
> Nature's chief and sweetest choir
> Him with cheerful notes admire;
> Chanting every day their lauds,
> While the grove their song applauds.
>
> Wake for shame, my sluggish heart!
> Wake and gladly sing thy part!
> Learn of birds, and springs, and flowers,
> How to use thy nobler powers.
>
> Call whole nature to thy aid,
> Since 'twas He whole nature made;
> Join in one eternal song,
> Who to one God all belong.[29]

The Bible makes it clear that there are practical results from this kind of worship. For one thing, we will take better care of God's creation and not waste or exploit it. We will learn to enjoy its beauty and wonder, and we ourselves will wonder at the God Who made it all and Who holds it all together.

Another result ought to be faithful stewardship of what God has given us. People who know how to worship the Creator will also know how to use their means in His service. I have a feeling that the proper worship of God the Creator could be a step toward solving some churches' budget problems. "The earth is the LORD's, and all its fullness" (Ps. 24:1). "The world is Mine, and all its fullness" (Ps. 50:12). David knew this truth, and this is why he said to the Lord, "For all things come from You, and of Your own we have given You" (1 Chron. 29:14). If we all worshiped the Creator as did King David, we would be as generous as he was.

Knowing the Creator is also a great help in practical Christian living. Paul quoted Psalm 24:1 *twice* in his discussion about Christian behavior (1 Cor. 10:23-29). God "gives us richly all things to enjoy" (1 Tim. 6:17), so we may use all things freely provided we do not cause somebody else to stumble, somebody who does not realize yet the bounty of God in creation. If we use God's creation to destroy one of God's children, then we are practicing idolatry and serving ourselves instead of worshiping and serving the Creator.

Your adoring response of worship to your Creator ought to help to cure you of worry. At least this is what Jesus taught in the Sermon on the Mount (Matt. 6:19-34). The rich worry because they have too much and are afraid they may lose it; and the poor worry because they do not have enough and struggle to secure what they need. Jesus did not give a lecture on budgets. Instead, He pointed to God's bounty in creation—His care of the birds and flowers—and then made His point: put God first, trust Him, and you will not have to worry.

> Wake for shame, my sluggish heart!
> Wake and gladly sing the part!
> Learn of birds, and springs, and flowers,
> How to use thy nobler powers.

"Remember now your Creator in the days of your youth," admonished Solomon as he brought Ecclesiastes to a close (Eccles. 12:1). Knowing and worshiping the Creator is a sure antidote to pessimism and cynical approach to life. The believer who sings the praises of the Creator is not likely to go around muttering, "Vanity of vanities, all is vanity" (Eccles. 1:2). Rather, he will join with Paul and shout, "Therefore, my beloved brethren, be steadfast, immovable, always abounding in the work of the Lord, knowing that your labor is not in vain in the Lord" (1 Cor. 15:58).

Finally, when we know and worship the Creator, we can face personal suffering and take it and use it for God's glory. "Therefore let those who suffer according to the will of God commit their souls to Him in doing good, as to a faithful Creator" (1 Pet. 4:19). Not a "faithful King" or even a "faithful Savior," but "a faithful Creator." Only a faithful Creator can make "all things work together for good" (Rom. 8:28). The climax of the book of Job—certainly a book about human suffering—comes when God reveals Himself as the Creator.

> Where were you when I laid the foundations of the earth?
> Tell Me, if you have understanding.
> Who determined its measurements?
> Surely you know!
> Or who stretched the line upon it? (Job 38:4–5)

As I look back, I can see how foolish I was to think that singing hymns to the Creator was unbiblical and even liberal! When you worship the Creator and lose yourself in the wonder of His creation, it can make a great difference in your personal Christian life.

THE WONDER OF THE REDEEMER

The wonder of God in creation is but the beginning. We must now consider the wonder of God in redemption.

> You are worthy to take the scroll,
> And to open its seals;
> For You were slain,
> And have redeemed us to God by Your blood
> Out of every tribe and tongue and people and nation,
> And have made us kings and priests to our God;
> And we shall reign on the earth. . . .
>
> Worthy is the Lamb who was slain
> To receive power and riches and wisdom,
> And strength and honor and glory and blessing!
> (Rev. 5:9, 10, 12)

Most of us feel very much at home with the theme of redemption, because the cross of Christ is central in our theology and our worship, and rightly so. "The atonement is the crucial doctrine of the faith," wrote Leon Morris. "Unless we are right here it matters little, or so it seems to me, what we are like elsewhere."[30] According to the hosts of heaven, the cross means *redemption*.

It is tragic when a believer loses the wonder of what it means to be redeemed. Dr. D. Martyn Lloyd-Jones once defined a Christian as a person "who is amazed at the fact that he is forgiven. He does not take it for granted."[31] One reason why we have baptism and the Lord's Supper is that we might be reminded of the price Jesus paid to save us. He has taken the wounds of Calvary to heaven with Him, perhaps to remind us *forever* that He died in our stead.

Twenty-eight times in the book of Revelation, Jesus is referred to as "the Lamb." The Greek word means "a little pet lamb," the kind you would not want to see slain for any reason. The major themes of Revelation are all related to the Lamb. God's wrath is "the wrath of the Lamb" (6:16). The tribulation saints are washed "in the blood of the Lamb" (7:14). The story is consummated with "the marriage of the Lamb" (19:7), and the church is "the bride, the Lamb's wife" (21:9). The heavenly throne is "the throne of God and of the Lamb" (22:1, 3). Eliminate the Lamb—redemption—from the book of Revelation and there is very little left!

We worship the Lamb, and wonder at the Lamb, because of Who He is. He is both human and divine, for He is "the Root of David" (Rev. 5:5) as well as the Lamb of God. This refers to our Lord's human Jewish ancestry (Isa. 11:1, 10). He has both humility and sovereignty, for He is "the Lion of the tribe of Judah" (Rev. 5:5; see also Gen. 49:8–10). He is both Redeemer and Ruler, Savior and Sovereign. The wonder of the nature of our Lord, His birth, life, and death, is enough to excite wonder in our hearts! Paul was right: "Without controversy great is the mystery of godliness: God was manifested in the flesh" (1 Tim. 3:16).

Consider John's symbolic description of the Lamb: "having seven horns and seven eyes, which are the seven Spirits of God sent out into all the earth" (Rev. 5:6). Seven, of course, is in the Bible the number of perfection. Here we have "seven horns," symbolizing perfect power; seven eyes, symbolizing perfect wisdom; and seven Spirits, symbolizing His perfect presence in all the earth. The Lamb is omnipotent, omniscient, and omnipresent!

We worship Him because of what He is and because of where He is—at the very throne of heaven. The Father is *on* the throne, and the Lamb is "in the midst of the throne" (v. 6). Jesus Christ stands in the center of that series of concentric circles that includes all the hosts of heaven. Jesus Christ is not on earth in a manger or a boat, or even on a cross. He is in heaven! He is at the center of heaven's worship! He is exalted "far above all principality and power and might and dominion, and every name that is named, not only in this age but also in that which is to come" (Eph. 1:21).

> O ye heights of heaven, adore Him;
> Angel hosts, His praises sing;
> All dominions, bow before Him,
> And extol our God and King;
> Let no tongue on earth be silent,
> Every voice in concert sing:
> *Evermore and evermore.*[32]

We worship Him not only for Who He is and where He is, but also what He has done for us. The fact that He was slain indicates that He first took upon Himself a human body, for God as spirit cannot die. When we worship the Lamb, we are bearing witness to the Incarnation as well as the Atonement. The word *slain* means "violently slain," reminding us of His suffering and sorrow.

His was a sacrificial death for the sins of the whole world, "every tribe and tongue and people and nation" (Rev. 5:9). When we worship the Lamb, we are bearing witness to the good news of the gospel that must be taken to the ends of the earth. As we shall discover in the next section of this pilgrimage, worship and witness must go together—and that witness must go to all nations. If a local congregation claims to be evangelical—that is, they worship the Lamb that was slain—but they are not evangelistic, there is something wrong.

The praise of the heavenly hosts recorded in Revelation 5 contains the elements of a balanced hymnal. They sang a gospel song about the blood of the Lamb that redeems sinners; they sang a missionary song about every tribe and tongue and people and nation; they reminded the church of its exalted position as kings and priests; and they even touched on future events: "we shall reign on the earth" (v. 10). This is a good model for us to follow if we want our worship to be balanced.

THE WONDER OF THE KING

The third worship scene is recorded in Revelation 11:15–18 where the emphasis is on praising Christ the King.

> We give You thanks, O Lord God Almighty,
> The One who is and who was and who is to come,
> Because You have taken Your great power and reigned.
> The nations were angry, and Your wrath has come,
> And the time of the dead, that they should be judged,
> And that You should reward Your servants the prophets and the saints,
> And those who fear Your name, small and great,
> And should destroy those who destroy the earth.
>
> (vv. 17, 18)

This is actually a hymn of thanksgiving, and the participants are praising Jesus Christ for three specific blessings.

First, they praise Him because He reigns supremely. This hymn was triggered by loud voices in heaven saying, "The kingdoms of this world have become the kingdoms of our Lord and of His Christ, and He shall reign forever and ever!" (v. 15). The King has taken His throne!

To be sure, Jesus Christ is reigning today as our Priest-King, seated on the Father's throne (Rev. 3:21). He is our Melchizedek, King of Righteousness and King of Peace (Heb. 6:20, 7:1–3). He graciously rules in the lives of willing believers and exercises His authority through His Word and His Spirit. But one day, He will exercise absolute authority when He takes His great power and reigns.

It is not too difficult for us to worship the King of Kings and Lord of Lords Who wore a crown of thorns for us. It is the next blessing that baffles us: they praise Jesus Christ because He judges righteously. He shall judge the rebellious nations, the death, and the destroyers of the earth.

Is it "spiritual" to praise a God of judgment? Personally, I do not know how we can avoid it! If we worship the Lamb that was slain, then we must believe in God's holy judgment of sin. If God could judge His sinless Son, Who became our substitute, why can He not judge sinful nations and rebellious sinners who destroy His earth? A sentimental view of the Cross leads to a sentimental view of sin; and the result is a condescending God Who is complacent toward sin and tolerant of sinners. But this is not the God Who elicits the praises of the hosts of heaven!

Many worshipers today would feel uneasy or perhaps embarrassed if asked to sing a song about judgment. (There are not too many of them in the average hymnal, so you need not get nervous.) We would classify hymns of judgment along with sermons like "Sinners in the hands of an angry God," museum pieces that are admired as theological antiques, but certainly not used in the open market.

For example, many hymnals contain John Cennick's hymn (adapted by Charles Wesley), "Lo! He Comes with Clouds Descending"; but some of the "judgment" verses are omitted. How would *your* congregation respond to these verses?

> See the universe in motion,
>   Sinking on her funeral pyre—
> Earth dissolving, and the ocean
>   Vanishing in final fire:
>   Hark the trumpet!
> Loud proclaims the Day of Ire!
>
> Graves have yawned in countless numbers,
>   From the dust the dead arise;
> Millions out of silent slumbers,
>   Wake in overwhelmed surprise;
>   Where creation
> Wrecked and torn on ruin lies![33]

Most of the songs about future events emphasize the more positive doctrines: the redemption of the human body, the reunion of God's people, and the life everlasting in heaven. Why praise the Lord because He is coming to judge? Because that is what the hosts of heaven do! In fact, all of nature anticipates the arrival of the Judge and deliverance from the bondage of sin.

> Let the heavens rejoice, and let the earth be glad;
> Let the sea roar, and all its fullness;

Let the field be joyful, and all that is in it.
Then all the trees of the woods will rejoice before the LORD.
For He is coming, for He is coming to judge the earth.
He shall judge the world with righteousness,
And the peoples with His truth. (Ps. 96:11–13)

If we are unmoved by the wonder of God's judgment, then either we have forgotten what sin is really like, or we have lost our vision of the holiness of God. It is not enough to preach, "God is love." We must also declare, "For our God is a consuming fire" (Heb. 12:29).

The third blessing that calls forth the praises of the heavenly hosts is the fact that Christ rewards righteously. He rewards His servants, not just the special ones (such as the prophets), but all the saints, small and great. They all have this in common: they fear His name. They stand in awe of God and His holy name, and by their faithful lives and service, they seek to honor that name.

THE WONDER OF THE BRIDEGROOM

The fourth worship scene focuses on the conquering Bridegroom and presents the great "Heavenly Hallelujah Chorus."

> After these things I heard a loud voice of a great multitude in heaven, saying, "Alleluia! Salvation and glory and honor and power belong to the Lord our God! For true and righteous are His judgments, because He has judged the great harlot who corrupted the earth with her fornication; and He has avenged on her the blood of His servants shed by her." Again they said, "Alleluia! Her smoke rises up forever and ever!" (Rev. 19:1–3)

Unable to remain silent, the elders respond with, "Amen! Alleluia!" And then a great multitude climaxes this heavenly "Hallelujah Chorus" with: "Alleluia! For the Lord God Omnipotent reigns!" (v. 6).

As far as I know, this is the only place in our Authorized Version where the Hebrew word *hallelujah* is not translated. Everywhere else it is given, "Praise the LORD!" The Hebrew word *hallelu* is an imperative meaning "Praise! Boast!"; and, when you add *Jah*, the name of God, you end up with *hallelujah*, "Praise Jehovah!" (The Greek is *alleluia*.)

The word *hallelujah* is used as an expression of rejoicing. The praise in Revelation 19 is in contrast to the lamentation in Revelation 18, where the world rulers mourn over the fall of Babylon. The heavenly hosts rejoice at the destruction of the harlot and at the marriage of the Lamb. Jesus Christ comes forth to conquer and to establish His righteous kingdom. "Let us be glad and rejoice and give Him glory, for the marriage of the Lamb has come, and His wife has made herself ready" (19:7).

The apostle John was so carried away by this heavenly worship that he fell at the feet of the angel and started to worship him! I wonder how many Sunday-morning worshipers in our churches today would be that stirred by the contemplation of the judgment of the world system, the victory of the King of Kings, the marriage of the Lamb, and the establishing of the kingdom? We are content to listen to Handel's "Hallelujah Chorus" once a year rather than sing our own hymn of praise to the King of Kings.

In this chapter, we have been cautiously considering the wonder of God: the Creator, the Redeemer, the victorious King, and the Conqueror. We have hardly scratched the surface of heaven's praise, and yet our hearts have been stilled and stirred by the wonder of God.

The better we know the Word of God, the better we shall know the God of the Word. Throughout Scripture, the wonder of God is revealed in both declaration and demonstration. "You are the God who does wonders" (Ps. 77:14). The God of creation is the God of redemption. He is the King Who reigns and the Conqueror Who defeats every enemy. The better we understand these wonders, the better we shall worship Him.

The substitute for the wonder of God is *idolatry,* the theme of the next stage of our pilgrimage.

HOLY FATHER,

I have been treading on holy ground!
Who would dare to contemplate the wonder of God!
Who would dare to listen to the worshiping hosts
    in heaven around Your holy throne!
Father, I confess that You are wonderful,
    in all that You are,
    in all that You do,
    in all that You say to me in Your word.
I see now how far short I come in my own personal worship—how much I
    have to learn.
Be patient with me!
Receive my worship, my praise, my thanksgiving,
    through Jesus Christ my Lord.
AMEN.

CHAPTER 6 *In which we think about idolatry and discover why it is so hateful to God*

UNTIL THEIR SEVENTY-YEAR sojourn in Babylon cured them, the Jewish nation was persistently guilty of idolatry. God's judgments on the false gods of Egypt did not make a lasting impression on Israel. In fact, more than once they expressed the desire to go back to Egypt! The repeated chastenings of the people, recorded in the book of Judges, apparently effected no lasting cure. First, God chastened them *in* their land, and then He took them captive *out of* their land. That finally cured them.

An idol is simply a substitute for God or a supplement to God. The Jews did not always abandon Jehovah for Baal or Chemosh or Molech. Often they gave Jehovah a place—even a prominent place—along with their other gods. But in putting Jehovah on the same level with the false gods, the people were robbing Him of His uniqueness and His glory. They were living by sight and not by faith. They were playing it safe and giving recognition to the gods of the enemy, just in case. And if they did totally abandon the worship of Jehovah for the worship of a false god, they were not only disobeying His divine law, but also defying His authority and denying His person.

Tourists who visit a pagan culture sometimes criticize the missionary for opposing idolatrous activities. "Why not just leave these dear people alone?" they argue. "Why change their picturesque culture, even if it does involve idolatry? Surely they can accept what they want from Christianity and work it into their own religion." We must be tolerant.

But God's declaration is unequivocal: "I am the LORD your God. . . . You shall have no other gods before Me" (Exod. 20:2, 3). This demand for exclusive worship is found not only in the law, but also in the historical books of the Old Testament (Elijah and the prophets of

Baal, 1 Kings 18), the psalms (Ps. 106), and especially the prophets (Isa. 46; Jer. 2). God did not "tolerate" the worship of other gods. He hated and despised it, and He chastened His people for practicing idolatry.

We who live today in a pluralistic society are prone to think that other religions may not be so bad after all. The people who practice them are good neighbors and fellow employees, and it would be difficult to believe that God would condemn them to hell just because they do not believe that Jehovah is the true God and Jesus Christ is His Son, the Savior of the world. The distinctions can get blurred, almost to the point that we start minimizing evangelism and missions.

Why was God so hard on the Jews when they apostasized and worshiped other gods? *Because their apostasy was threatening the very plan He had for bringing salvation to the whole world.* It was not a matter of one religion being better than another. It was purely a matter of one religion—Judaism—being the *only* true faith. Paul summarizes Israel's privileges perfectly in Romans 9:4, 5: "to [Israel] pertain the adoption, the glory, the covenants, the giving of the law, the service of God, and the promises; of whom are the fathers and from whom, according to the flesh, Christ came, who is over all, the eternally blessed God. Amen."

And they abandoned all of that just to be like their neighbors! The prophets compared their sin to adultery: they were unfaithful to the God Who loved them and "married" them when they entered into covenant relation with Him. "They have forsaken Me, the fountain of living waters, and hewn themselves cisterns—broken cisterns that can hold no water" (Jer. 2:13).

Thus, the sin of idolatry had personal, national, and international consequences. The individual worshipers were robbing themselves of the richness of their spiritual heritage, and this was affecting their character and conduct. The nation was not fulfilling its God-ordained purpose in the world, to be a light to the Gentiles and a revealer of the glory of the true God. As a result, the other nations were left without a clear witness. It was through His *blessings* that God wanted Israel to witness to the nations, but their sins robbed them of blessing. In the end, it was His *chastening* that got the message across to the Gentiles. Jerusalem became a byword among the nations.

THE USELESSNESS OF IDOLS

The contrast between the true God and the idols is seen vividly in Psalm 115, a Passover psalm. Accustomed to bowing before idols, the Egyptians no doubt were perplexed, perhaps even amused, that the Jews worshiped no visible gods.

> Not unto us, O LORD, not unto us,
> But to Your name give glory,
> Because of Your mercy,
> Because of Your truth.
> Why should the Gentiles say,
> "So where is their God?"
>
> But our God is in heaven;
> He does whatever He pleases.
> Their idols are silver and gold,
> The work of men's hands.
> They have mouths, but they do not speak;
> Eyes they have, but they do not see;
> They have ears, but they do not hear;
> Noses they have, but they do not smell;
> They have hands, but they do not handle;
> Feet they have, but they do not walk;
> Nor do they mutter through their throat.
> Those who make them are like them;
> So is everyone who trusts in them.
>
> (Ps. 115:1-8)

There is more than subtle irony here. The psalmist is reminding the Jewish worshiper of the losses that he will incur if he does not worship the true and living God.[34]

"They have mouths, but they do not speak." *No promises.* The God of Israel spoke to them through Moses, Joshua, Samuel, David, and the prophets. He gave them covenants and promises that were never shared with the Gentile nations (Eph. 2:11-12). Imagine what it would be like to have to live without God's promises!

"Eyes they have, but they do not see." *No protection.* "I will guide you with My eye" (Ps. 32:8). "The eyes of the LORD are on the righteous" (Ps. 34:15). Peter quoted that promise in his first letter

(1 Pet. 3:12); and if any man knew what it meant to have the protection of God, it was Peter!

"They have ears, but they do not hear." *No prayer*. Our God hears us when we pray. He encourages us to come to Him and pour out our hearts before Him. Moses prayed on the mountain, and Joshua in the valley defeated Amalek (Exod. 17:8–16). When Israel sinned, Moses made his way to the top of Sinai and there interceded for the people. What would it be like to live for God, or to serve God, without the privilege of prayer?

"Noses they have, but they do not smell." *No praise*. "And the LORD smelled a soothing aroma" (Gen. 8:21). Coming from the burnt offerings that Noah had laid on the altar. This is a human illustration of a divine truth—the theologians call this "anthropomorphism"—but the truth is obvious: God delights to have His people worship and praise Him and bring Him their best. When Paul received the missionary offering from the church at Philippi, he did not see food, money, and warm clothing. He saw "a sweet-smelling aroma, an acceptable sacrifice, well pleasing to God" (Phil. 4:18). What would it be like to worship a dead idol and know that your best was never recognized or received?

"They have hands, but they do not handle." *No power*. "Do not be afraid of them," said Jeremiah of the false gods, "for they cannot do evil, nor can they do any good" (Jer. 10:5). Then he asked, "Are there any among the idols of the nations that can cause rain?" (14:22). Elijah's ridicule of Baal only exposed the impotence of this false god: "Cry aloud, for he is a god; either he is meditating, or he is busy, or he is on a journey, or perhaps he is sleeping and must be awakened" (1 Kings 18:27).

"Feet they have, but they do not walk." *No presence*. Isaiah contrasted Jehovah Who carried Israel with Bel and Nebo who had to be carried by their worshipers (Isa. 46:1–7)! One of the names of our Savior is "Immanuel . . . God with us" (Matt. 1:23). Our Lord's farewell promise was, "Lo, I am with you always, even to the end of the age" (Matt. 28:20). Even in the darkest valley, our God is with us (Ps. 23:4).

"Those who make them are like them; so is everyone who trusts in them." *No progress*. Idolatry is basically worshiping and serving "the creature rather than the Creator" (Rom. 1:25); and only the Creator can transform us to be like Himself. If the psalmist is correct, and I think he is, then those who worship false gods eventually become blind, deaf, dumb, weak, and immobile—spiritually speaking. If we become like the god we worship—whether material or imaginary—we can never rise above the god that we manufacture for ourselves. It is a vicious circle that only redemption can break! It is a dangerous thing to worship false gods. Instead of transformation, you experience retrogression, the deadening effects of false worship.

MODERN IDOLATRY

How easy it is for us to judge the Jewish nation for its idolatry, and yet be blind to the same sin in our own nation and churches today! In the name of so-called modern science we have eliminated the Creator from His creation, leaving the creature to play God in the world. Alienated from the God Who made him in His image, man tries to be both Creator and creature; and with every problem he solves, he creates three or four new ones. No wonder the world today faces an ecological crisis that seems insoluble. Instead of exercising dominion over the earth (Gen. 1:26-30), man is destroying the earth; and one day God will judge him for doing it (Rev. 11:18).

If the church today were truly worshiping the Creator and not the creature, we Christians would be making better use of the precious resources God has given us. The church would be speaking out against such sinful waste, and would also be setting the right kind of example. If we really believed that we are stewards of God's glorious creation, and if we praised Him sincerely for these bountiful gifts, we would never waste them, abuse them, or use them selfishly. If God rejoices in His works (Ps. 104:31), then He must be deeply grieved by our works in destroying His creation.

Whatever we try to use *for God* that has in some way been divorced *from God* can only become a barrier between us and God. In Jeremiah's day, the people of Judah and Jerusalem boasted of their temple and felt confident that what went on there would guarantee security for the nation; but the prophet called the building "a den of thieves" (Jer. 7:11). "Do not trust in these lying words, saying, 'The temple of the LORD, the temple of the LORD, the temple of the LORD are these'" (7:4). The building had become an idol, and the priestly ministries in the building were but empty ceremonies. No wonder God permitted the invading Babylonians to destroy it.

I receive a great many letters from pastors and church leaders, and I have noticed that many of the church letterheads have on them pictures of church buildings. This is also true of Sunday bulletins: on the cover, there is usually a picture of the church building. You will probably find the same pictures on the literature that promotes the ministry of the church. Why? Because we identify the "church organism" with the "church organization" that meets in the "church building." We forget that the "church" is made up of people, not brick and mortar.

We also tend to measure success in terms of real estate. Resources that perhaps ought to go into hands-on ministry too often are channeled into buildings that stand empty most of the week. If the average commercial business used its resources and facilities that carelessly, it would go broke. Is it possible that our mania for religious real estate is but a subtle form of idolatry?

I am not suggesting that a growing church family should not have adequate facilities. I am saying that, in many cases, building committees get their values confused and their vision blurred. As Vance Havner once said, "What should have been a mile-stone becomes a mill-stone."

What does this have to do with worship? A great deal! The wonder of God includes the wonder of the Creator Who has given dominion to man. We cannot worship God acceptably and waste and destroy His creation. In most cases, as far as modern man is concerned, the treasures of creation are represented by money. You and I are not likely to burn down a forest or spill oil in a lovely lagoon, but we may support that kind of evil by the way we spend our money, even for "religious" things.

If worship transforms individuals and churches—and it does, if it is spiritual worship—then one of the evidences of this transformation will be seen in the way these individuals and churches use God's gifts in creation. It is not enough to sing on Sunday morning "This is my Father's world" and then live the rest of the week as though *we* were in charge. This is idolatry. This is turning God's house into a den of thieves.

What is a "den of thieves"?

It is the place that thieves run to *when they want to hide!*

Yes, you and I can actually use *worship* to cover up the idolatry that God sees in our hearts! But true worship, that "adoring response" to all that God is and does, simply must alter a person's values. When you meet God, your view of His world, of other people, and of yourself, is bound to change.

It is time that we met some of these people.

FATHER IN HEAVEN,

You are the true and living God,
   and I worship You! I adore You!
Deliver me from the worship of substitutes.
May I worship the Creator,
   not the creation or the creature.
May I worship the Redeemer,
   not the experience of redemption
   or the blessings it brings to my life.
Tear from my heart every idol!
May I worship and serve You and You alone.
   Through Jesus Christ, Your Beloved Son,
AMEN.

CHAPTER 7 *In which we meet some believers who met God and worshiped Him*

THE WONDER OF God is seen perhaps most vividly when we enter into the experiences of people just like ourselves who met God and worshiped Him. No two experiences are alike and no two persons are identical. This is a great encouragement to me, because I am prone to want to imitate what others have experienced. After all, if God did it that way for Jonathan Edwards or Charles Spurgeon, He can certainly do it that way for me!

Of course He can—but that is not always His plan. I am a unique person to Him and He wants me to have a unique experience. To be sure, all worship experiences have some elements in common, but they also have their own special features that may not be duplicated in the lives of others. Each of us is different and our worship experiences are bound to be different.

The mistake we make is in imitating the *accidentals* instead of the *essentials*. "Once, as I rode out into the woods for my health," wrote Jonathan Edwards, "having alighted from my horse in a retired place . . . I had a view that for me was extraordinary, of the glory of the Son of God, as Mediator between God and man, and his wonderful, great, full, pure and sweet grace and love, and meek and gentle condescension."[35] What an experience that must have been! Perhaps I could duplicate that experience if only I had a horse to ride and a woods to ride him in.

"The wind blows where it wishes," Jesus told Nicodemus, "and you hear the sound of it, but cannot tell where it comes from and where it goes" (John 3:8). We can harness the power of the wind, but we cannot write a formula that will accurately predict and control the wind. "So is everyone who is born of the Spirit," our Lord added.

70

God is infinitely original in His workings and we had better refrain from locking Him into a formula.

I want you to meet several Bible characters who personally met God, and I want us to learn from their experiences what is involved in true spiritual worship. Please do not make the mistake of thinking that any one of these persons experienced *all* that a believer could experience, or that one saint's experience was greater than that of another. Their experiences were tailor-made for them, just as your worship experiences are tailor-made for you. We are not meeting these people so we can imitate them or duplicate their experiences. We are meeting them so we can learn from them some of the elements that make up true worship that pleases God.

ABRAHAM

The Hebrew word *shāchāh*, which means "to bow down, to worship," is first used in the Bible in Genesis 18. Abraham is resting in his tent door in the heat of the day (and it can get very hot in the Holy Land!) when he sees three strangers approaching his camp. This is unusual, because travelers do not journey when the sun is hot; but the aged man jumps up and runs to meet them. Abraham discovers that his visitors are the Lord and two of His angels! Abraham "ran from the tent door to meet them, and bowed himself to the ground" (Gen. 18:2).

As you read this chapter, you see Abraham illustrating two aspects of worship. In the first half of the chapter, he is busy as the *servant* of God; and in the last half, he is standing still and conversing as the *friend* of God. As believers, we are both servants and friends (John 15:15); and both are essential for a balanced worship experience.

Worship and service go together; in fact, it is difficult to conceive of worship apart from service. "You shall worship the LORD your God, and Him only you shall serve" (Matt. 4:10). In spite of his age and the heat of the day, Abraham immediately served the Lord, and he did it personally, even though he could have called any one of hundreds of servants. Note the verbs: he *ran* (v. 2); he *hurried* (v. 6), he *ran* again (v. 7). Note that he ordered the very best for his Lord: "fine meal" (v. 6) and "a tender and good calf" (v. 7). It was not until his Lord was served that Abraham rested: "and he stood by them under the tree as they ate" (v. 8).

Service is worship if we are serving the Lord and giving Him our best. Abraham had often worshiped the Lord at his altar, and offered up his choicest sacrifices; but now he was *personally* worshiping Him by serving Him a meal.

But the last half of the chapter records a contrasting scene. Abraham is not running here and there; he is standing quietly before the Lord, talking with Him about the situation in the cities of the plain. "Shall I hide from Abraham what I am doing?" asked the Lord (v. 17). "No longer do I call you servants," said Jesus to His disciples, "for a servant does not know what his master is doing; but I have called you friends, for all things that I have heard from My Father I have made known to you" (John 15:15).

It is the same man, Abraham, in both scenes; and it is the same Christ receiving his worship and service. Abraham *the servant* was in a hurry; Abraham *the friend* stood and waited. The servant involved others—Sarah, the young man who prepared the meat—but the friend stood before the Lord *alone*. The servant gave his best to the Lord; the friend asked for God's best for others.

The key word is *balance*. We are expected to lose ourselves in contemplation or give ourselves in ministry. We are His servant-friends, ministering to Him and fellowshiping with Him. Both are essential to true worship. Abraham was burdened for Lot and, I believe, for the lost sinners in Sodom and Gomorrah. Should not the blessing of worship lead the burden of intercession and witness?

A second worship experience for Abraham is described in Genesis 22, the offering up of his only son, Isaac, on the altar. "Stay here with the donkey," he told the two servants; "the lad and I will go yonder and worship, and we will come back to you" (v. 5). It seems incredible that Abraham could look upon this greatest of all tests as an act of worship. Do we today consider our times of suffering and deep pain as experiences of *worship*? To do so certainly ought to deepen for us both the experience of suffering and the experience of worship.

Our time of suffering can indeed be experiences of worship if we will do what Abraham did. To begin with, *he focused on God's promises and not on explanations*. God had promised that Isaac would be the heir and that through him a great nation would be built. Abraham believed this promise and knew that one of two things would happen: either God would not require Isaac to be slain, or He would raise the dead son and give him life (Heb. 11:17–19). Abraham worshiped a God big enough to handle the contradictions inherent in the situation. The whole enterprise seemed unnatural, unreasonable, and unbelievable. It could only be handled by faith through worship.

Abraham also focused on *God's power, not human resources*. He had experienced God's resurrection power in his own life (Rom. 4:18–21), and he believed that this same power could also work in Isaac's life. Abraham had plenty of resources, for he was a wealthy man, but nothing he possessed could meet the need at the altar. Only God could do that!

Finally, Abraham focused on *God's purposes and not his own personal desires*. As a result, Abraham ended up with a deeper experience of love, a clearer vision of God, a greater dependence on God, and a wider promise of blessing to others. It was worth it all!

Believers today try every remedy possible in dealing with their sufferings and sacrifices. Perhaps it is time we tried *worship*. Because Abraham looked upon this entire experience of trial as one of worship, God enabled him to obey by faith and win the victory. The purpose of worship is not that we might escape suffering, or merely endure it. The purpose of worship is that we might glorify God by enlisting our suffering and using it creatively.

Worship is a transforming experience, and it can even transform suffering into glory. But if Abraham had not worshiped God at the altar and the tent door, he could never have offered Isaac as he did and see trial transformed into triumph. A crisis does not make a man; it shows what a man is made of. The character of a man or woman of God is built day by day, in the worship-and-serve experiences of life. Then, when the crisis comes, we find ourselves spiritually prepared; and suffering can marvelously become an act of true worship.

Abraham teaches us that worship is an everyday experience, and that sincere service to God is an act of worship. "Assuredly, I say to you, inasmuch as you did it to one of the least of these My brethren, you did it to Me" (Matt. 25:40). But worship that is service must be balanced by worship that is quiet and solitary, worship that is concerned for others. Serving, communing, suffering: these are some i gredients in our worship experience. Blessed is the believer who is balanced and who knows when it is time to serve, to commune, to suffer.

JACOB

More than one liturgical writer has used Jacob's experience at Bethel (Gen. 28) as a model for true worship. While I do not think it is the only model, or even the most important model, I do believe it teaches us some important truths about worship that too often are overlooked.

When Jacob met God at Bethel, he was running away from home and trying to run away from his problems. He certainly was not seeking God! Yet God came to him and revealed Himself to Jacob in a singular way. Worship must always be an experience of God's grace. If anything, God should have abandoned Jacob and let him "stew in his own grease." Jacob had plotted with his mother, lied to his father, and stolen from his brother. He was hardly a qualified candidate for a high and holy experience of worship!

God graciously breaks in on us when we least expect it—or even deserve it. When worship ceases to be an experience of grace it ceases to be an experience of glory, for grace and glory must go together. Jacob was the most unlikely person to have this experience, and he had it at the most unlikely time, in the most unlikely place. That is the grace of God!

Jacob's experience at Bethel transformed his life. Yes, it took another thirty years before he really began to live like a man who knew God; but this was the beginning. Jacob reminds me of the modern "successful man" that the world admires: self-assured, confident, able to manipulate people and circumstances, clear in his goals, willing to walk on others (and lie if necessary) to achieve those goals. Jacob knew how to take care of himself and defend himself, but he did not know how to change himself. God had to do that for him.

He had a threefold experience at Bethel: he saw a vision, he heard a voice, and he made a vow. Centuries later, Isaiah the prophet would have a similar experience, and so would Peter the apostle as he sat on a housetop in Joppa.

Jacob saw a vision of a staircase between heaven and earth. On the staircase, the angels were coming and going. At a time when he felt alone and afraid, Jacob discovered that God was with him and that heaven and earth were not far apart! He may have been sleeping with a hard stone for a pillow, but while he was asleep, God's angels were serving him! He was not alone and there was no reason for him to be afraid.

We know from John 1:51 that this vision is a picture of our Savior: "Most assuredly, I say to you, hereafter you shall see heaven open, and the angels of God ascending and descending upon the Son of Man." He is God's living link between a holy heaven and a sinful earth. Man cannot build a tower to reach to heaven, but God can *and did* build a bridge between heaven and earth. God was reconciled to Jacob, but Jacob had to be reconciled to God—and to his family.

The transforming power of worship is not experienced in its fullness immediately. It took God nearly thirty years to get Jacob to the place where he was yielded to God's will and not manipulating people and circumstances to fit his own schemes. God is patient.

Jacob saw a vision and realized that he was not alone, that God was with him and for him. Jacob heard a voice—the voice of God—that assured him of God's purpose and blessing. There was no word of reproach; instead, it was God's gracious word of promise. "Behold, I am with you and will keep you wherever you go, and will bring you back to this land; for I will not leave you until I have done what I have spoken to you" (Gen. 28:15). You and I as believers today will not hear that audible voice, but we can claim as valid a promise as the one God gave to Jacob: "I will never leave you nor forsake you" (Heb. 13:5). We might add: "being confident of this very thing, that He who has begun a good work in you will complete it until the day of Jesus Christ" (Phil. 1:6).

What was Jacob's "adoring response" to this revelation of God's grace and glory? He made a vow, and this happens to be the first vow recorded in the Bible. Overcome with fear, Jacob realized that he was at the very house of God (*beth-El*), the gate of heaven. What he thought was a dead-end street was actually the gate of heaven, opening into a new life under the watchful care of God.

Jacob thought he was alone, but God was there. He thought he was facing a bleak future, yet God gave him new purpose and new promises to encourage him. Whether Jacob's vow was another "bargain" or not, we need not discuss; good and godly Bible scholars disagree. It is enough to note that the schemer was starting to break down and acknowledge his need for God; and Jacob's vow is a confession of his first steps of faith. It was indeed the dawning of a new day and the beginning of a transformed life; and it started with worship.

JOB

Job's initial response to the first wave of trials was to humble himself and worship. "Then Job arose, tore his robe, and shaved his head; and he fell to the ground and worshiped" (1:20). He was even able to say, "Blessed be the name of the LORD" (1:21). But in his subsequent discussion with his three friends, Job gradually lost the attitude of worship and began to challenge God. He never questioned God's right to bless him or chasten him; what perplexed Job was that his suffering seemed out of proportion to the benefits that anyone was receiving.

As the discussion continued, Job began to accuse God of keeping a safe distance so that His servant could not present his case. God indeed was the Judge, but He was absent from the courtroom; and Job could not present his arguments to Him!

Then God showed up—and Job had nothing to say. "Behold, I am vile; what shall I answer You? I lay my hand over my mouth" (Job 40:4).

After listening to God's lecture on natural theology, Job had to confess,

> I know that You can do everything,
> And that no purpose of Yours can be withheld from You,
> You asked, "Who is this who hides counsel without knowledge?"
> Therefore I have uttered what I did not understand,
> Things too wonderful for me, which I did not know. . . .
>
> I have heard of You by the hearing of the ear,
> But now my eye sees You.
> Therefore I abhor myself,
> And repent in dust and ashes.

(Job 42:2-3, 5-6)

Job's worship experience warns us that right theology is no guarantee of right relationship with God. God is always greater than our mental images of Him and our doctrinal formulas. Zophar was right: "Can you search out the deep things of God? Can you find out the limits of the Almighty?" (11:7). "Behold, God is great," affirmed Elihu, "and we do not know Him . . ." (36:26).

I have a feeling that Job would say a hearty "Amen!" to the admonition written by Solomon in Ecclesiastes 5:1, 2—"Walk prudently when you go to the house of God; and draw near to hear rather than to give the sacrifice of fools, for they do not know that they do evil. Do not be rash with your mouth, and let not your heart utter anything hastily before God. For God is in heaven, and you on earth; therefore let your words be few."

"What we utter before God must come from the heart," wrote Matthew Henry, "and therefore we must not be rash with our mouth, never let our tongue out-run our thoughts in our devotions; the words of our mouth must always be the product of the meditation of our hearts. Thoughts are words to God, and words are but wind, if they be not copied from the thoughts."[36]

No wonder Job put his hand over his mouth!

ISAIAH

Isaiah 6 is the *locus classicus* for the study of worship. In fact, some writers have made it *the* biblical passage almost to the exclusion of others like Genesis 28, Exodus 34, and even Revelation 1, 4, and 5. While Isaiah's worship experience can say a great deal to us, we must not overdo it; nor must we insist that the Christian worshiper today duplicate his experience in exactly the same way.

We are not sure where Isaiah had this transcendent vision of Jesus Christ enthroned in heaven (see John 12:41). Perhaps he was in the temple; we do not know. Since Isaiah prophesied during the reign of King Uzziah (Isa. 1:1), this vision could well have taken place while the king was still alive. To attempt to relate the empty throne on earth with the throne in heaven, where God sat in glory, is to read something into the text that Isaiah never put there. Nor should we spiritualize the scene and say, "Perhaps something in my life has to 'die' before I will see Christ in all His glory." Uzziah was likely alive when Isaiah had this life-transforming experience, and the king simply died that same year.

Isaiah had a fourfold experience of worship; and in this sense, his experience relates to us today: he saw something—Christ in glory; he heard something—the heavenly praises; he felt something—the cleansing power of God; and he did something—he volunteered for difficult service.

Rather unexpectedly, *Isaiah saw something*. He saw "the Lord sitting on a throne, high and lifted up . . ." (Isa. 6:1). John informs us that the prophet saw Jesus Christ (John 12:41). Isaiah discovered the reality of the invisible world of the spiritual. It was a mystical experience in the best sense of the word: the invisible became visible and the spiritual became real. It was a vision of the glory of God and the holiness of God. No matter what might happen to the throne on earth, the throne of heaven was secure. "God reigns over the nations; God sits on His holy throne" (Ps. 47:8).

You and I today are not apt to experience this same kind of vision, but we can still behold the glory of the Lord with the eyes of the heart through the pages of the Word (Eph. 1:18). "Grace is but glory begun," wrote Jonathan Edwards, "and glory is but grace perfected."[37] Jesus saw God's glory in the flowers of the field and in the faces of little children. Sometimes in the Word, sometimes in nature, sometimes in a special experience of life, perhaps even a difficult experience, we see the glory of God and our hearts are lifted up in worship. "Open your eyes," said the mystic Jacob Böhme, "and the whole world is full of God."[38]

Isaiah also *heard something*, the voices of the heavenly creatures as they praised God. The Hebrew word *seraph* comes from a root meaning "to burn," suggesting that the seraphim are the guardians of the blazing holiness of God. One creature cried to the other as the antiphonal praise rang through the throne room of heaven: "Holy, holy, holy is the LORD of hosts; the whole earth is full of His glory!"

As the seraphim praised God, the doorposts shook and the heavenly temple was filled with smoke, suggesting the judgment of God (Ps. 74:1). Isaiah saw a vivid portrayal of the holiness of God, His holy throne, His justices and holy judgment against sin.

God's holiness is His divine perfection, that which makes Him unique and separated from anyone else and everything else. God is set apart; He is separate. The prophet immediately sensed his own sinfulness and openly confessed it to the one Whom he knew as the Holy One of Israel (see 5:19). The angelic beings could praise God because their lips were pure, but Isaiah's lips were unclean and he was a man undone.

It is a good thing when our vision of God's holiness leads us to the confession of our own sinfulness. The prophet had pronounced "Woe!" on the sinners in Judah (5:8, 11, 18, 20, 21, 22); but now he was pronouncing "Woe!" upon *himself*. It is not enough in our worship only to see the Lord; for if we truly see Him as He is, we will also see ourselves as we are.

Isaiah saw something and heard something, but he also *felt something*. One of the seraphim interrupted his worship to bring Isaiah the cleansing that he needed. It is not enough to see the throne; we must also see the altar, the place of sacrifice for sins. A throne without an altar would mean conviction and condemnation, not cleansing.

The prophet felt the live coal, but that was not all; he also received the word of forgiveness: "Your iniquity is taken away, and your sin is purged" (v. 7). That worship experience is incomplete— and vulnerable—which brings about conviction but not cleansing. Satan the accuser would like nothing better!

It is unfortunate that we have minimized the importance of feelings in our experience of worship. We preach about presenting our bodies as a living sacrifice (Rom. 12:1, 2), but then we want to anesthetize our nervous system and eliminate normal emotional responses. Our churches are filled with icy people like Michal, David's wife, who criticized her husband because he was too fervent in his worship (2 Sam. 6:20). While we certainly want to avoid shallow emotionalism, we dare not grieve the Holy Spirit in our desire to be "proper." I want to feel something within as I worship God—a sense of glorious wonder, a joyful acceptance, a brokenness for sin, an empowering of His Spirit, a release from burdens and shackles— whatever it is He has for me as I come before His holy throne.

We dare not manufacture religious feelings, or seek to duplicate the experiences of the great saints of God. But neither should we quench the Spirit (1 Thess. 5:19) and tell Him what He can and cannot do. If our hearts are sincere, if we know the Word of God, and if we are yielded to the Spirit, we will experience just what God wants us to experience, and He will be glorified. To be sure, we must be alert to the fact that there are false spirits that want to give us a spurious experience of worship; and we must "test the spirits" to make sure we are not being deluded (1 John 4:1–6).

If Isaiah's experience stopped here, it would not be true spiritual worship. The prophet went on, however, to *do something:* he surrendered himself to God for His special service. "Here am I! Send me" (v. 8). His experience began with *sight*—he saw the Lord. It led to *insight*—he saw himself as a defiled sinner. But the end result was *vision*—he saw the need and volunteered to do the work God wanted him to do. Worship led to service, as true worship must always do.

If worship is a transforming experience, then it must result in service that transforms the world. It was while Paul and Barnabas were ministering to the Lord at Antioch that God called them to carry the gospel to the Gentiles (Acts 13:1–3). The Greek word translated *minister* means "to perform a priestly service." Like Isaiah, Paul and Barnabas had a worship experience that transformed them into missionaries.

The nation needed the Word, and God needed a man. Both needs were met when Isaiah, a worshiper, said, "Here am I! Send me!" Perhaps there would be more volunteers today if our churches were engaged more in spiritual worship. A recent mailing from one evangelical mission board informs me that they need over three hundred workers for twenty-three different fields!

ENTER TO WORSHIP—DEPART TO SERVE! is a sign I often see over the doors of church buildings, and I agree with it completely. If we have sensed the holiness and glory of God, and if we have felt the joy of sins forgiven, then we are ready to go out to serve Him, no matter how difficult the task. "The previous experiences made Isaiah quick to hear God's call," wrote Alexander Maclaren on this text, "and willing to respond to it by personal consecration. Take the motive-power of redemption from sin out of Christianity, and you break its mainspring, so that the clock will only tick when it is shaken. It is the Christ who died for our sins to whom men say, 'Command what Thou wilt, and I obey.'"[39]

EZEKIEL AND DANIEL

The worship experiences of the prophets Ezekiel and Daniel were unique. They saw visions, they felt the hand of God, and they heard the voice of God; and often their experience of God left them prostrate. Daniel's receiving of prophetic truth actually made him ill, and Ezekiel's visions aroused the enmity of some of the other Jews. It was not easy for either of these men to worship God; they paid a price.

I rarely participate in "prophetic conferences," not because I question either their content or intent, but because I often fail to detect that necessary ingredient of worship. The emphasis is on God's "program" and not God's Person. The book of the Revelation is frequently presented as the revelation of future events, and not, as it is in truth, "the revelation of Jesus Christ."

When worship and prophecy are divorced, the result is mere religious curiosity; and this often leads to division. Ezekiel and Daniel saw God, not a prophetic chart, and it cost them something to see Him. The prophets were men who knew God and therefore had the right to pull back the veil and look into the future. Even John the apostle was personally overwhelmed as he witnessed the unfolding drama of God's redemptive plan, to the point of falling down to worship the angel who was guiding him!

In my library, I have at least four shelves of books devoted to prophecy. Few of them emphasize worship. Even some of the commentators on Revelation either minimize or ignore the worship emphasis of that exciting book. Commenting on the numerous worship hymns in Revelation, the late Dr. Merrill Tenney wrote: "In these expressions may be found the essence of worship which pervades the entire Apocalypse. They breathe a sense of awe at the power of God exercised in judgment, and a deep gratitude for the work of redemption."[40]

If we keep worship central in our prophetic studies and preaching, then we will have an easier time keeping our priorities straight. We will see future events in the light of God's glory and grace, and not just His divine government. We will stop debating over less important details and start seeing the "big picture" that reveals the greatness of God. If the study of prophecy makes me want to argue instead of worship, there is something wrong with my studies.

Early in my ministry, I preached a long sermon about the coming of Christ, into which I packed everything I thought I knew about prophecy. A pastor friend was in the congregation that evening, and he said to me after the service, "I think you told me more about prophecy than I really wanted to know! Frankly, I've moved off of the Program Committee and now I'm on the Welcoming Committee." I got the point.

I am not likely to have the same visions and revelations as Ezekiel and Daniel, since these two devoted prophets have recorded their experiences for my learning. But I do want to cultivate the same worshipful attitude as the prophets, so that I am indeed glorying in Jesus Christ and not boasting of my prophetic insight. I want to be on the Welcoming Committee.

MARY OF BETHANY

We must not overlook Mary of Bethany and the worship experience she had at the feet of Jesus. Here is the record:

> Then six days before the Passover, Jesus came to Bethany, where Lazarus was who had been dead, whom He had raised from the dead. There they made Him a supper; and Martha served, but Lazarus was one of those who sat at the table with Him. Then Mary took a pound of very costly oil of spikenard, anointed the feet of Jesus, and wiped His feet with her hair. And the house was filled with the fragrance of the oil.
>
> But one of His disciples, Judas Iscariot, Simon's son, who would betray Him, said, "Why was this fragrant oil not sold for three hundred denarii and given to the poor?" This he said, not that he cared for the poor, but because he was a thief, and had the money box; and he used to take what was put in it.
>
> Then Jesus said, "Let her alone; she has kept this for the day of My burial. For the poor you have with you always, but Me you do not have always." (John 12:1–8)

Mark adds these significant words:

> "She has done what she could. She has come beforehand to anoint My body for burial. Assuredly, I say to you, wherever this gospel is preached in the whole world, what this woman has done will also be told as a memorial to her." (Mark 14:8–9)

Mary's experience was right in her own home. By her devotion to Christ, she transformed her home into a temple. We get the impression that she caught the guests by surprise, although it is likely that her brother and sister knew of her plans. She gave lavishly of her costly gift, and she did it because she loved her Lord deeply.

She did what she did in order to please Jesus Christ and not to impress the disciples. Because it was for Him, Mary did not count the cost. Cheap worship that only seeks to "get by" could never win the approval of the Lord. Mary had the same attitude of heart that motivated David: "I will not take what is yours for the LORD," he told Ornan, "nor offer burnt offerings with that which costs me nothing" (1 Chron. 21:24). The minute we start to count the cost, we stop worshiping God sincerely.

The image of "fragrance" is a good one for worship, for it illustrates some of the beautiful aspects of worship that are often ignored. Is there anything useful or helpful in a lovely fragrance? To be sure, perfume can cover the offensive odors that sometimes come along, but in the house at Bethany there were no such odors. If anything, the house probably was filled with the fragrance of delicious food!

The person who worships, who gives his or her best, brings a fragrance to life, indefinable, perhaps even mysterious, so that ordinary places become fragrant with the presence of Christ. The priest who burned the incense daily at the golden altar was bound to pick up some of that fragrance and carry it with him wherever he went.

Because of her unselfish act of worship, Mary brought joy to the heart of the Master. He was pleased with what she did. The blessing spread throughout the house. It brought out the best in Mary and the worst in Judas! She was unmoved by the disciples' criticism (they all agreed with Judas!), because her only desire was to please Jesus Christ.

The beauty and fragrance of her act of worship did not stop in the little home in Bethany. The blessing has spread throughout the whole world! And it has continued to spread wherever the Word of God is shared with people. *Never underestimate the blessed consequences of one adoring act of worship!* Your private devotions in your own home can have spiritual repercussions around the world.

"For we are to God the fragrance of Christ among those who are being saved and among those who are perishing" (2 Cor. 2:15). When we give ourselves to Him in worship, we are sharing the fragrance with Him and with others. We are releasing a spiritual perfume that can bring joy to people we will never meet until we arrive in glory.

This brief survey of the worship experience of a select group of Bible personalities reminds us that God is interested in variety. Each experience is different, just as each person is different. We today are not required to duplicate their experiences, but we are expected to give the same kind of devotion to the Lord. No worship experience was final; there was always something more to learn and to do. The accidentals must remain in history; we dare not imitate them. The essentials have belonged to God's people since Adam built his first altar.

We must focus on God and not on an experience.

We must be sincere, open, and honest with Him.

We must give our best, and do so because we love Him.

We must look beyond events and experiences to see God and the work He has for us to do.

We must be willing to pay the price to get to know God better.

The wonder of God must excite us and humble us! But so must the wonder of the church, which is the subject of our next chapter.

GRACIOUS FATHER,

As I read about the experiences of Your people as they worshiped You, my heart and my soul cry out for You!

Lord, I don't want to imitate their experiences. I do want to learn from them the joyful blessing of worshiping You and entering more deeply into the wonder of it all.

May I never be satisfied with myself or with my worship. Help me to hunger and thirst after righteousness! Help me to seek after You with all my heart!

May the fragrance of Christ cling to me. May it spread. May I be a blessing to the ends of the earth because I have worshiped You in spirit and in truth.

Through Jesus Christ,
AMEN.

CHAPTER 8 *In which we discover the wonder of God's church*

THE GREATEST WONDER that God has on earth is the wonder of His church.

> One holy Church of God appears
> Through every age and race,
> Unwasted by the lapse of years,
> Unchanged by changing place.
> SAMUEL LONGFELLOW[41]

Accustomed as we are to criticizing the church, we need to remind ourselves that God's people are precious to Him and that He delights in their corporate worship. As important as our private worship is, it must be balanced by congregational worship; and this is where the church comes in. In this age of individualism, we must heed the words of Evelyn Underhill: "The corporate life of worship . . . checks religious egotism, breaks down devotional barriers, obliges the spiritual highbrow to join in the worship of the simple and ignorant, and in general confers all the supporting and disciplining benefits of family life."[42]

THE CHURCH IS ONE

When I was being examined for ordination, I was asked to define the "invisible church." In my youthful brashness, I replied, "The invisible church is what meets on Sunday evening." Personally, I dislike the terms "visible church" and "invisible church," but even more I dislike "true church" as opposed to the "local church." While no local church is perfect, it can at least strive to be "true."

You and I know that only God can see His church as it now exists

in heaven and on earth. What we see is a mixture of good and bad,
wheat and tares; and the more the church becomes like the world, the
more difficult it is to distinguish between the real and the counterfeit.
However, with all of its spots and wrinkles, the church is still the
Body of Christ in this world, the worshiping community that seeks to
"proclaim the praises of Him who called [them] out of darkness into
His marvelous light" (1 Pet. 2:9).

The Christian who echoes the slogan of the sixties, "Jesus, yes!
The church, no!" does not know what he is saying. It is impossible to
separate the redeemed from their Redeemer, the flock from the Shepherd, the members of the Body from their exalted Head. Timothy
Dwight was fully aware of the sins and weaknesses of the church, but
still he wrote:

> I love Thy kingdom, Lord,
> The house of Thine abode,
> The Church our blest Redeemer saved
> With His own precious blood.

The wonder of the church is not that we are a *perfect* people, but
that we are a *purchased* people. God thinks enough of us to redeem us
with "the precious blood of Christ, as of a lamb without blemish and
without spot" (1 Pet. 1:19). In spite of our defilement and division,
we are still "a chosen generation, a royal priesthood, a holy nation,
His own special people" (2:9). That is the wonder of it all!

Too often we have a narrow view of God's church. We see only
our congregation, or perhaps only our denomination. If we belong to
an "independent" church (another term I dislike), we may revel in
our so-called independence and forget that no believer can be independent of other believers; for we belong to the same Body and therefore belong to each other. There is certainly nothing wrong with a
local church being autonomous and self-governing if it so desires, but
it must not cultivate an "independent" attitude.

Why? Because an independent attitude can lead to pride, and
pride often leads to criticism and competition. I once asked the pastor
of a large church if he ever prayed publicly for any other church in the
city, and he replied, "I wouldn't dare! My people think our church is

the *only* church in town!" We are prone to wonder how their worship of God is viewed in heaven when they have such an exclusive attitude.

The Body of Christ never meets on earth, but each local assembly is witness to the fact that there is such a thing as the Body of Christ on earth. I can sin against the church of Jesus Christ either by ignoring it completely and settling for private worship, or by fellowshiping and worshiping with an independent spirit and an exclusive outlook. If I harbor the feeling that my group is the only "true church," then my worship will grieve the Spirit of God and run headlong against the teaching of the Word of God.

This is not to say that all churches are created equal. They are not. There are some congregations whose doctrine and practice are so unbiblical that the faithful believer would not want to be identified with them. But we must be careful to "judge nothing before the time" (1 Cor. 4:5). Only God sees the truth about each assembly. The church at Smyrna thought it was bankrupt, but Jesus said it was rich; while the church at Laodicea thought it was rich and the Lord announced that it was "wretched, miserable, poor, blind, and naked" (Rev. 2:9; 3:17).

John Calvin came to the conclusion that "the distinguishing marks of the church" are the preaching of God's Word and the observing of the sacraments, or ordinances.[43] To make church government, liturgy, or methods of ministry tests of faith and fellowship would mean going beyond the boundaries set by Scripture.

What does this mean to our worship of God? Simply this: we must worship as those who recognize the greatness of the church and the glory of this spiritual temple that Christ is building. Just as we set aside one day for special worship, and thereby consecrate *all* places, so we meet in one assembly of our choice, and thereby acknowledge *all* assemblies.

If you ever start to lose the sense of the glory and wonder of the church, just review the many images of the church that God gives in His Word. In his book *Images of the Church in the New Testament*, Paul Minear lists nearly one hundred similes and metaphors that illustrate the church and various aspects of its ministry. No one image says it all. The church is so wonderful that the Spirit used dozens of images to tell us what it is like.

It is unfortunate that churches have a tendency to emphasize only one or two of these rich images. Some congregations see themselves only as a body, a family, or perhaps an army—and this attitude helps to determine their outlook and ministry. They forget that the church is also a priesthood, a flock following the Shepherd, and an athletic team that must strive for the goal. What we need is balance, not only in our views of the church but also in our public worship.

Sometimes we gather as a family and our worship is that of submissive children who love their Father. On other occasions we are an army, and we find ourselves praying with the early church, "Lord, You are God, who made heaven and earth and the sea, and all that is in them. . . . Now, Lord, look on their threats, and grant to Your servants that with all boldness they may speak Your word" (Acts 4:24, 29). There are also times when the church comes as a bride, expressing love for her Lord and Savior, and simply enjoying His fellowship. Blessed is that worship leader who knows the times and the seasons and is able to discern which image best fits the congregation at a given time.

The Church Is Organized

The church is both an organism and an organization, and we dare not separate the one from the other. After all, if an organism is not organized, it will die. Paul and his associates organized churches; they did not leave behind nebulous groups of people who lacked order and leadership. As I read the book of Acts and Paul's epistles, I get the impression that Paul was afraid lest structure get in the way of ministry. It seems that the organizational structure was somewhat adaptable and that the churches avoided drawing organizational charts. They depended more on "networks" than on charts, with each believer discovering his or her gifts and putting them to work where they were most needed.

Even a cursory review of church history reveals that God has blessed every form of church government and the men who were involved in them. He is doing so today. Let each believer be fully persuaded in his own mind—and let him give the same freedom to others that they give to him. The important thing is that God's church is organized and that everything is "done decently and in order" (1 Cor. 14:40). Too much emphasis on organization produces an institution; too little emphasis may produce chaos. The believers at Corinth grieved the Spirit by their disorder, but the saints in Thessalonica were in danger of quenching the Spirit by their overemphasis on order. Again, what we need is balance.

THE CHURCH IS ACTIVE

We have grown so accustomed to the assembly of God's people that we have lost the wonder of it all. Just stop to consider what really happens—or should happen—when the people of God meet together for the worship of God.

To begin with, *congregate*. Other groups in our locality also meet together, but their meeting has little in common with the gathering together of God's people. They meet temporarily as individuals, but we are a part of a permanent union with Jesus Christ, a spiritual union that wipes out all distinctions. "There is neither Jew nor Greek, there is neither slave nor free, there is neither male nor female; for you are all one in Christ Jesus" (Gal. 3:28). This is a miracle!

We congregate because Jesus Christ is alive and coming again. We meet on the Lord's Day, the day of resurrection. In the old creation, God worked for six days and then rested, setting aside the seventh day as a memorial of the completion of the old creation. But in the new creation, the church, Jesus Christ finished His work on the cross, rested on the seventh day, and then arose from the dead on the first day of the week. Every time a church assembles on the Lord's Day to worship, it is bearing witness that Jesus Christ is alive. We are also bearing witness that He is coming again—"not forsaking the assembling of ourselves together, as the manner of some, but exhorting one another, and so much the more as you see the Day approaching" (Heb. 10:25).

We not only congregate, *we celebrate*. We do something together. What we do might be planned, a regular ritual that is accepted and understood; or what we do might be spontaneous and unplanned. The heart of celebration is that we lift our hearts to God and express to Him our love and thanksgiving. "Oh come, let us sing to the LORD!

Let us shout joyfully to the Rock of our salvation. Let us come before His presence with thanksgiving; let us shout joyfully to Him with psalms" (Ps. 95:1, 2).

True spiritual celebration delivers us from "services as usual." To be sure, we need to guard against the "evangelical exhibitionist" who uses a worship service just to show off. But we also need to watch out for the worshiper who is so caught up in formalism and routine that there is no sincere celebration at all. He merely goes through the motions. Both extremes should be avoided.

Just about everything the assembled church does can be classified as celebration: singing, giving thanks, sharing in the offering, encouraging one another, reading and hearing the Word of God. It all depends on the spirit in which it is done. If the worship service is platform-centered, then we will be only spectators at a religious performance. But if there is true worship and celebration, then we will be participants, sharing our praise with the Lord and with His people.

The wonder of the church is that its celebration never grows old. There is always a "new song" to sing to the Lord because we have experienced new grace, discovered new truth, or been reminded in a new way of the blessing of God.

We congregate, we celebrate, and *we commemorate*. At the Lord's Table we remember His death, resurrection, and coming again. In baptism, we are reminded of the price He paid for us that we might receive the gift of the Spirit and become a part of the body of Christ. Congregations that follow the Christian Year commemorate the great events of sacred history: our Lord's birth and baptism; His death and resurrection; the coming of the Holy Spirit after His ascension, and so forth. These key events never grow old, but take on new meaning year after year.

We also *communicate*. In the preaching of God's Word, the truth is communicated to His people; and in the singing of the hymns and gospel songs, the truth is likewise communicated by choir and congregation. As we shall discover in a later chapter, true worship involves witness: to God, to the church, and to the lost world.

When we gather to worship, we also *consecrate*. Attendance at worship indicates that we have consecrated our time to the Lord. Sharing in the offering means we have consecrated our means to the Lord. Those who use their gifts and talents in a special way in the service have consecrated them for the Lord's use. Before the worship ends, we consecrate ourselves to go forth into the world to serve others in the name of Christ. "Here am I, Lord! Send me!"

I find, too, that there are times in a worship service when I must *contemplate* what God is saying to me. "Let the words of my mouth and the meditation of my heart be acceptable in Your sight, O LORD, my strength and my redeemer" (Ps. 19:14). I appreciate it when the worship leader gives me time to think. Some worship services are so crowded that there is no time for silence and for meditation. One pastor I know introduced a one-minute silent prayer into the service, and several members of the church complained about it. They admitted that they had nothing to think about for that long a time!

THE CHURCH IS WONDROUS

When we lose the wonder of the church, then what we do as a part of the congregation will be boring and routine. We need to enter the congregation with that sense of awe that God has privileged us, *even us*, to be a part of His church! "Who am I, O Lord GOD? And what is my house, that You have brought me this far?" (2 Sam. 7:18). If we come with open, seeking hearts, the Lord will meet us and satisfy our needs.

Sometimes I go to church to worship as one of His sheep, desperately needing the care of the Shepherd. "We are His people and the sheep of His pasture" (Ps. 100:3). At other times, I worship as a member of the Body, seeking to draw from Him the spiritual energy I need for ministry, and also seeking to minister to others in the Body. Yes, there are occasions when I share in worship as a soldier in His army, wounded from the battles of the previous week. There are also those times (and how I wish there were more of them!) when I simply love Him as a part of His Bride, and experience the inner joy and satisfaction that spiritual love can give. I recall with shame that there was a time when I criticized "sentimental Christianity," the kind expressed by the mystics. I have learned that my emotions must be a part of worship, otherwise a part of me is not yielded to the Lord.

The wonder of the church is the miracle of variety, vitality, and unity as together we worship the Lord. As we yield to His Spirit, there is that exciting element of spontaneity that makes each time of worship special. When our worship services are predictable, the Spirit is not at work in His fullness. This is not to suggest the absence of planning, for the Spirit can direct a worship leader a week in advance as well as during the meeting; but it does suggest that we make room for the heavenly wind to blow and keep the windows open.

Moses said it perfectly:

> Happy are you, O Israel!
> Who is like you, a people saved by the LORD,
> The shield of your help
> And the sword of your majesty!
> Your enemies shall submit to you,
> And you shall tread down their high places.
> (Deut. 33:29)

Yes, we ought to be a happy people for we are indeed a privileged people. To think that God has called us to be a part of His people, a holy congregation that has been assembling for worship for centuries! In spite of its divisions and its spots and blemishes, the church is *God's* church and we are privileged to worship Him. What a wonder is the church! It has survived persecutions from without and problems from within. It has been attacked by its enemies and neglected by its friends, and yet it has survived. Infected with heresies, stained by compromises, and weakened by selfishness and poor leadership, it somehow has endured and still bears witness in the world.

This centuries-long continuity of worship is a part of our rich heritage as Christians. Though circumstances and liturgies change, one thing remains constant: God's people assemble to praise and worship Him. What a thrill to realize that we are a part of that "great celebration" that has included Augustine, Luther, Calvin, Woolman, Spurgeon, and Wesley!

What a wonder is His church! With all of its faults, it is a transforming fellowship that can change our lives and through us change society.

GRACIOUS FATHER,

I confess that many times I enter Your house and join Your people with a heart that lacks wonder. I take it all for granted.
Forgive me!

Help me to see the wonder of Your church. May I see Your church as a miracle of Your grace. May I never get accustomed to my blessings as a part of Your family, Your people.

Help me to realize that Your church is much bigger than the assembly in which I fellowship. May I see how wide Your love is!

Grant, O Lord, that I shall add to the vitality of the church and not be a hindrance to the work of Your Spirit. May I see the great variety You have put into Your church, and may I not be afraid of encountering something new.

I pray in Jesus' Name,
AMEN.

PART III

Worship Involves Witness

In the average church service the most real
thing is the shadowy unreality of everything.
The worshipper sits in a state of suspended
mentation; a kind of dreamy numbness
creeps upon him; he hears words but they
do not register, he cannot relate them to
anything on his own life-level.
A. W. TOZER[44]

And with great power the apostles gave
witness to the resurrection of the Lord
Jesus. And great grace was upon them all.
ACTS 4:33

CHAPTER 9 *In which we learn what it means to witness to God*

3Bld celebration - Edification - proclamation

3F

WHEN THE CHURCH gathers to worship, it also gathers to witness. That witness is threefold: to the Lord, to the church itself, and to the world. In other words, balanced worship includes celebration (witness to the Lord), edification (witness to one another), and proclamation (witness to the world). Of these three, the most important is our witness to the Lord. If that is not right, then we will not be able to edify one another or evangelize the lost.

We do not go to church to worship, because worship ought to be the constant attitude and activity of the dedicated believer. We go to church to worship *publicly* and *corporately*. What we have been doing privately, for the most part, all week long, we do publicly as we gather with the people of God on the Lord's Day. Each worshiper brings to the service his or her own spiritual contribution of blessing, depending on the personal walk with the Lord.

God does not need our worship. "Nor is He worshiped with men's hands, as though He needed anything, since He gives to all life, breath, and all things" (Acts 17:25). God does not need our worship, but He does seek our worship and invite us into His presence. God dwells in an atmosphere of worship: "The host of heaven worships You" (Neh. 9:6). Yet He invites sinful man to come and worship Him! And He paid the dreadful price necessary for us to be able to "draw near with a true heart in full assurance of faith, having our hearts sprinkled from an evil conscience and our bodies washed with pure water" (Heb. 10:22).

But what does God do while we worship? He knows all things, so our worship does not surprise Him. He owns all things, so our gifts do not enrich Him. He is perfect in all His attributes, so our fellowship with Him cannot improve Him. What, then, does our worship

97

do for God? When we witness to Him in praise, prayer, and giving, what is accomplished in heaven?

We may not be able to explain it, but the Bible declares that God delights in His people and responds to their worship and obedience. God is not the prisoner of His own attributes; He is free to respond to His creation and His children. "May my meditation be sweet to Him," prayed the psalmist (104:34), suggesting that God is pleased when we think about Him. God's divine nature is not affected by our worship, but His response and relationship to us are certainly affected. God was delighted in David, but He took His Spirit away from Saul.

God is a Person, and our worship involves a personal relationship to Him and a personal response from Him. He is not a static Being Who is "imprisoned" or "paralyzed" by His own attributes or divine purposes. "But our God is in heaven; He does whatever He pleases" (Ps. 115:3). God interacts with us as we seek Him, worship Him and serve Him. In ways that we cannot fully understand, He even enters into our sufferings and sorrows. "In all their affliction He was afflicted" (Isa. 63:9). The orthodox theologians tell us that God is self-existent and self-sufficient; and they are right. But when God brought creation into being, especially man, made in the image of God, He had to *relate to it and respond to it*. Certainly He rejoiced at creation when He saw it was very good, and certainly He rejoices when His people love Him and praise Him.

I must add here a caution that we not make the mistake of the "process theologians" who tell us that our worship personally enriches God so that He then becomes a "better God" as He is evolving toward perfection. Nothing we do can add anything to God's essential nature which is changeless. In His essence, God does not change; but in His relationships and responses, He does change. It is we who are enriched by worshiping Him.

Another caution: even the sincere worship we present to the Lord must first come from Him and be generated by His Spirit in our hearts. "For all things come from You, and of Your own we have given You" (1 Chron. 29:14). "We pursue God," wrote A. W. Tozer, "because, and only because, He has first put an urge within us that spurs us to the pursuit."[45] The priests in the tabernacle offered sacrifices on an altar whose fire was ignited from heaven.

SPIRITUAL SACRIFICES

God's people today are "a holy priesthood, to offer up spiritual sacrifices acceptable to God through Jesus Christ" (1 Pet. 2:5). Exodus 29 describes the consecration of the Old Testament priests, a ceremony that typifies the spiritual experience of believers today. The priest was cleansed with water, and we have been washed and made clean (1 Cor. 6:9–11; Titus 3:5). He was clothed with special garments, and we have been clothed in the righteousness of Christ (2 Cor. 5:21; see also Isa. 61:10). The oil was applied to his right ear (hear God's Word), right thumb (do God's work), and right great toe (walk in God's way), illustrating the ministry of the Holy Spirit to us. "But the anointing which you have received from Him abides in you" (1 John 2:27).

"Spiritual sacrifices" are not necessarily nonmaterial, although some of them are. The word means "of a spiritual quality, related to the Spirit." If what we offer is given sincerely to God, in the Spirit, through Jesus Christ, then our gifts are acceptable as spiritual sacrifices. It is the character and attitude of the giver that gives value to the offering. The poor widow's copper coins brought more joy to the Lord than did the rich worshipers' expensive sacrifices (Mark 12:41–44).

When the church is at worship, giving witness to God, what are the spiritual sacrifices that we should bring?

OURSELVES

Perhaps the first and the most important is *ourselves as living sacrifices*. "I beseech you therefore, brethren, by the mercies of God, that you present your bodies a living sacrifice, holy, acceptable to God, which is your reasonable service" (Rom. 12:1). Under the old covenant economy, the worshiper brought a live animal to be slain; it was a dead sacrifice. But under the new economy of grace, we are *living* sacrifices, able to serve the Lord and glorify Him.

Two men in the Bible illustrate what it means to be a living sacrifice—Isaac (Gen. 22) and Jesus Christ. Isaac was a young man when he went with his father Abraham to Mount Moriah and there was offered as a sacrifice. Isaac was willing to die so that he and his father might be obedient to the Lord. He did not die, of course, because God's purpose was to test Abraham's love, not take his son. When Isaac was unbound and taken from that altar, it was like a resurrection from the dead (Heb. 11:17–19). Isaac was from that moment on a living sacrifice.

But our Lord actually died and arose from the dead. There was no substitute provided for him as for Isaac, because He *was* the substitute. When our Lord came forth from the tomb, He still bore on His body the marks of the nails. He became a living sacrifice, and He remains a living sacrifice in glory today. His sacrifice for sin was completed; now He lives to minister to His people and perfect them in holiness (Heb. 13:20, 21).

Note, then, the characteristics of a person who is a living sacrifice: obedient to the Father; willing to yield everything; no arguing or complaining; no explanations needed; raised to enter into a new kind of life; ministering to others.

Early in this worship pilgrimage, we discussed Romans 12:1, 2, so there is no need to repeat that discussion here. You will recall that God wants us to give Him our body, mind, and will; and that He renews the mind and transforms the life when we present ourselves as living sacrifices. I like to do this each morning when I go to my study for my devotional time. By faith, I give my Father my body, mind, and will, just as the Old Testament priest presented that burnt offering to the Lord early each morning.

How does this apply to corporate worship? If my body belongs to the Lord, then I ought to be present when God's people gather to worship. All of the faculties of my body should be open to His blessing and available for His service. I should see to it that I am at my best on Sunday morning, and this might mean saying no to late-night activities on Saturday evening. If worship is important to me, then I will take care of my body and present it to God as a living sacrifice for His glory.

PRAISE

If I have presented my body to God in worship, then I must use that body to glorify Him; and this is where prayer and praise come in.

"Therefore by Him let us continually offer the sacrifice of praise to God, that is, the fruit of our lips, giving thanks to His name" (Heb. 13:15). This is what the hosts of heaven are doing now and what we shall all be doing forever in glory.

We often say that "talk is cheap," but God takes our words seriously. Even our idle words will be judged by God (Matt. 12:36), because what we say with our lips really comes from the heart. It is a dangerous thing to praise God with lips and yet have a heart that is far from Him (Matt. 15:7-9). The word for this is *hypocrisy.*

God accepts the sincere praise from our lips as though it were an expensive sacrifice. "I will praise the name of God with a song, and will magnify Him with thanksgiving. This also shall please the LORD better than an ox or bull, which has horns and hooves" (Ps. 69:30, 31). "Let them sacrifice the sacrifices of thanksgiving, and declare His works with rejoicing" (107:22). "Accept, I pray, the free-will offerings of my mouth, O LORD" (119:108).

If my praise is to be an acceptable spiritual sacrifice, it must come from my heart; and it must be voluntary, not forced. It must be a "freewill offering." I have a tendency to resist the efforts of worship leaders to get me to "sing louder." In fact, there are times when we may not want to sing and when we must depend on God's grace to enable us to sing (Col. 3:16). It is one thing to praise God in heaven and quite something else to praise Him in prison (Acts 16:25) or before going out to die on a cross (Matt. 26:30). That takes grace!

It has been my experience that sacrifice and true praise usually go together. Many of David's choicest psalms grew out of difficult situations, as did some of the great hymns of the church. True praise is not cheap; it is costly. "And when the burnt offering began, the song of the LORD also began . . ." (2 Chron. 29:27). Sacrifice and song really belong together. True praise is costly.

And true praise ought to be continual: "let us continually offer the sacrifice of praise to God" (Heb. 13:15); "I will bless the LORD at all times; His praise shall continually be in my mouth" (Ps. 34:1). The person who does not find beauty in his or her own backyard is not likely to find it in some distant place; and the Christian who cannot praise God anywhere, at any time, is not likely to praise Him in a worship service. We do not go to church to praise God: we bring our praise with us. The worship service should not be an interruption of our praise, but rather a continuation and augmentation of our praise, as we join hearts and voices with other believers.

PRAYER

Prayer is another spiritual sacrifice that we offer to God through Jesus Christ. "Let my prayer be set before You as incense, the lifting up of my hands as evening sacrifice" (Ps. 141:2). The reference here is to the altar of incense, the golden altar, that stood before the veil in the holy place of the tabernacle and temple. Each morning and evening, when the priest trimmed the lamps, he would burn incense on the golden altar, the only offering that was permitted on that altar. It was to be "a perpetual incense before the Lord" (Exod. 30:8). According to Revelation 5:8 and 8:3, 4, incense symbolizes "the prayers of the saints."

There were two altars in the tabernacle: a brazen altar at the door, where the sacrifices were offered; and a golden altar by the veil, where the incense was burned. You could not get to the golden altar without first coming to the brazen altar, the place where the blood was shed. We come to God and "enter the Holiest by the blood of Jesus" (Heb. 10:19). Furthermore, you could not get to the golden altar without stopping to wash at the laver, that large brass basin that stood between the door and the veil. "If I regard iniquity in my heart, the Lord will not hear" (Ps. 66:18). In other words, the true worshiper must come to God through the blood of Christ and with clean hands and a pure heart. Otherwise, all prayer and praise is futile.

The fact that God commanded a *golden* altar shows how important prayer is to Him, and its position next to the holy of holies shows its importance even more. If prayer is important to God, then it ought to be important to us.

The priest had to prepare himself for this ministry. He was required to use a special blending of fragrant spices (Exod. 30:34, 35) *and nothing extra*. The fire for burning the incense had to come from the brazen altar (Lev. 16:12) where the blood was shed. Any "strange fire" would invite the judgment of God, as would using the special incense for any other purpose (Exod. 30:37).

Do we prepare ourselves to pray? I am not thinking of those

"emergency prayers" that we send up to the throne when we are in danger. I am thinking about our daily prayers, our public prayers, our prayers of worship and adoration. Too often they are shallow and routine, simply because we have not prepared ourselves to pray and to worship. Of course, the best way to prepare to pray is to live a life of prayer. "Prayer at its best is the expression of the total life," wrote A. W. Tozer. "All things being equal, our prayers are only as powerful as our lives."[46]

But prepared incense is useless without the fire, and this is where the Holy Spirit comes in. "When thou prayest," wrote John Bunyan in his quaint way, "rather let thy heart be without words, than thy words without heart." Only the Holy Spirit can ignite the fire in the heart so that our prayers are ascending like incense. "I have never found any who prayed so well as those who had never been taught how," said Madame Guyon. "They who have no master in man, have one in the Holy Spirit."[47]

Charles Spurgeon told his pastoral students that he thought that true preparation for prayer consisted in "the solemn consideration beforehand of the importance of prayer, meditation upon the needs of men's souls, and a remembrance of the promises which we are to plead . . ."[48] Good counsel, indeed, not only for pastors but for all believers.

The posture of the body is not as important as the posture of the soul, the submission of the inner person to the Lord. David "sat before the LORD" when he prayed (2 Sam. 7:18), while the Pharisee and tax collector stood in the temple to offer their petitions (Luke 18:9–14). It is proper to kneel (Ps. 95:6 and Eph. 3:14), to fall prostrate (Mark 14:35; Matt. 26:39), and to lift your hands to the Lord (1 Tim. 2:8). Sometimes our praying is quiet communion; at other times, we find ourselves "laboring fervently. . . in prayers" like Epaphras (Col. 4:12).

The important thing is that we look upon our praying as a sacrifice presented to the Lord. We want to give Him our best.

SERVICE AND GIVING

"But do not forget to do good and to share, for with such sacrifices God is well pleased" (Heb. 13:16). Here we have the sacrifice of service and the sharing of material goods. We do not do good works in order to earn God's acceptance, nor do we bring material gifts (usually money) in order to purchase God's blessing. The sharing of ourselves and our possessions with others is evidence that we have already trusted Christ and are members of His family. "Now all who believed were together, and had all things in common" (Acts 2:44).

Christian service must be an act of worship; otherwise, it will become a terrible burden. Whether we are teaching the Word, singing in the choir, sweeping the floor, or visiting the sick and lonely, our motive must be to please and glorify the Lord. Once we start to worry about the criticisms or praises of men, we will become intimidated and lose the glory that belongs to those who serve Him for His pleasure alone.

Christian giving must also be an act of worship, whether we are putting an offering envelope in the plate or sharing our home with a visiting missionary. When the Philippian church sent Paul a missionary gift, he saw their sharing as an act of worship and their gift as a beautiful sacrifice to the Lord. "Indeed I have all and abound. I am full, having received from Epaphroditus the things sent from you, a sweet-smelling aroma, an acceptable sacrifice, well pleasing to God" (Phil. 4:18).

Too often our giving is motivated by guilt instead of grace. "So let each one give as he purposes in his heart, not grudgingly or of necessity; for God loves a cheerful giver" (2 Cor. 9:7). Giving comes from the heart, and the heart of giving is the recognition of the grace of God. Giving becomes an act of worship when it comes from our heart and when we give only to please God. If more of God's people would learn the meaning of spiritual worship, there would be plenty of money to meet the needs of ministries at home and overseas.

The prophet Malachi delivered his message to a group of priests who were not giving God their best. They were bored with their service ("What a weariness!"), and they were putting imperfect sacrifices on the altar. "And you bring the stolen [which cost them nothing!], the lame, and the sick; thus you bring an offering!" (1:13). "And when you offer the blind as a sacrifice, is it not evil? And when you offer the lame and sick, is it not evil? Offer it then to your governor! Would he be pleased with you? Would he accept you favorably?" (1:8). And yet Sunday by Sunday, God's people bring offerings to the

Lord that they would be embarrassed to give their family or friends as birthday or Christmas gifts!

It is interesting to see the different ways that churches use for receiving offerings. One church I pastored had boxes at the exits and the worshipers dropped their gifts in as they entered the sanctuary. Most churches pass offering plates or collection bags. Some congregations march past offering plates or collection bags. Some congregations march past the communion table and drop their offerings in plates. However it is done, the offering must be an act of worship as we bring our spiritual sacrifices to the Lord.

A Broken Heart

Perhaps the most costly of the spiritual sacrifices is the one David mentions in Psalm 51:16, 17—"For You do not desire sacrifice, or else I would give it; You do not delight in burnt offering. The sacrifices of God are a broken spirit, a broken and a contrite heart—these, O God, You will not despise."

David's broken heart was not self-pity or temporary regret over his sins and the suffering that he brought to himself and others. It was the result of deep repentance. As you read Psalm 51, you see that David saw his sins in the light of God's grace and goodness, and this broke his heart. It is not the badness of man that leads us to repentance; it is the goodness of God. "Or do you despise the riches of His goodness, forbearance, and longsuffering, not knowing that the goodness of God leads you to repentance?" (Rom. 2:4). It was when the prodigal son thought of the bounty of his father's table that he repented and went back home.

God's warning to Israel in the past, and to the church today, is, "Do not harden your hearts!" This is one of the major themes of the book of Hebrews: "Today, if you will hear His voice, do not harden your hearts" (3:7, 8, 15; 4:7). Saints with hard hearts cannot worship God and please Him. Their worship is but a comfortable religious routine that leaves them farther from God than when they started. The scribes and Pharisees were very religious men who were careful about their duties, yet they grieved the Lord Jesus by the hardening of their hearts (Mark 3:5).

What are some of the marks of a hard heart? An unwillingness to admit and confess my own sins. A bitter spirit toward another believer. An unwillingness to forgive. A resistance to the Word of God. An inflexible attitude that cannot be taught or changed. A feeling that my way is the right way and the only way. A fear of change and an unwillingness to learn new things. A refusal to let people get "too close." A touchiness of spirit, a supersensitive attitude that makes it difficult for people to get along with me. Being preoccupied with my own needs and not being concerned about the needs of others.

God has some special blessings for those who cultivate a broken spirit and a broken and contrite heart. "'Heaven is My throne, and earth is My footstool. Where is the house that you will build Me? And where is the place of My rest? For all those things My hand has made, and all those things exist,' says the LORD. 'But on this one will I look: on him who is poor and of a contrite spirit, and who trembles at My word'" (Isa. 66:1, 2).

"The LORD is near to those who have a broken heart, and saves such as have a contrite spirit" (Ps. 34:18). "He heals the brokenhearted and binds up their wounds" (147:3).

"For thus says the High and Lofty One who inhabits eternity, whose name is Holy: 'I dwell in the high and holy place, with him who has a contrite and humble spirit, to revive the spirit of the humble, and to revive the heart of the contrite ones'" (Isa. 57:15).

When we worship God as we should, we bring to Him a broken heart and a humble spirit. The more we worship, the more our hearts are humbled before Him. There is no room for pride in the presence of the Lord. Abraham stood before the Lord and saw himself as "dust and ashes" (Gen. 18:27). Isaiah saw himself as an unclean man with unclean lips, and Job cried out, "I am vile!" (Job 40:4). When Simon Peter saw the blessing of God, he fell down before Jesus and cried, "Depart from me, for I am a sinful man, O Lord!" (Luke 5:8). Some of God's choicest gifts are for those who know the blessing of a broken heart.

Witnessing To God

Worship involves witness, and witness begins with our witnessing to God. We bring to Him our "spiritual sacrifices" and offer them with gratitude to Him. In so doing, we glorify Him and we edify ourselves and others. It is this ministry of edification—the by-product of celebration—that is the subject of our next chapter.

GRACIOUS FATHER IN HEAVEN,

I confess that I have often brought to You sacrifices that were unworthy. Instead of bringing the firstfruits, I brought the leftovers. Instead of bringing what really cost me something, I brought You the easiest and the cheapest thing.

Forgive me!

Help me to see that all of life is an opportunity to present spiritual sacrifices to You. My words and my works are just as much offerings to You as my wealth.

What a privilege it is to be one of Your priests! Help me to minister as I should, and may my spiritual sacrifices please You.

Through Christ our Lord,
AMEN.

CHAPTER 10 *In which we learn what it means to witness to one another*

IF WORSHIP HAD only a vertical dimension and we witnessed only to God, then our pilgrimage would end here. But worship has a horizontal dimension: we witness to one another in the church and to a lost world outside the church. It is not enough that *I* am transformed by worship; I must also help to transform *others*, and I should allow others to be used by God to transform me. One of the tests of a spiritual gathering is whether or not we leave it better persons than when we entered it. "I do not praise you," Paul wrote to the Corinthians, "since you come together not for the better but for the worse" (1 Cor. 11:17).

In my own pilgrim journey, there have been high and holy hours when I came away from the worship service having seen the glory of God and heard His voice speaking specifically to me. One such time was a seminary chapel when the president's message burned its way into my soul and confirmed in me my calling to preach the Word. Another occasion was a Sunday-school gathering where the youthful speaker, without knowing it, put iron into my soul and fortified me to continue ministering in a difficult place.

I recall a midweek service when, after giving the message, I sat down in the front pew and began to weep. It had been a difficult week, and I felt as though I could never take another one. The people gathered around me, encouraged me, prayed for me, and the Lord broke through the clouds and caused the sun to shine.

Even now, as I look back over more than thirty-five years of ministry, I can hear the hymns and see the faces of the worshipers in services where God touched my life. Too often, like Thomas, we miss the meeting and lose the blessing.

108

THE MINISTRY OF EDIFICATION

What are the saints supposed to do when they get together to worship God? Nowhere in the Bible are we given an order of service. First Corinthians 14:26 is perhaps the closest thing we have to a description of what went on in the apostolic church: "Whenever you come together, each of you has a psalm, has a teaching, has a tongue, has a revelation, has an interpretation. Let all things be done for edification." Our problem today is just the opposite: when we come together, very few of us have *anything* to share! If a minister wants to quiet down a meeting, one of the best ways is to ask for personal testimonies or words of edification.

Perhaps we have been so wrapped up in the *content* of the worship service that we have neglected the *intent*. I must confess that I am not at all stirred by the discussions of the liturgists when they debate ancient orders of service, defending one against another. The problem of form versus function has challenged the church since the election of the first deacons (Acts 6). When structure starts to get in the way of ministry, it is time to make sensible changes. That there is one divinely ordained order of service that all of us must obey, few liturgists will claim. That there are patterns and principles, learned both from Scripture and church history, all will affirm.

Bishop J. C. Ryle found at least seven necessary elements for a Christian worship service: (1) the honoring of the Lord's Day; (2) ministers leading the people; (3) the preaching of the Word; (4) public prayer; (5) the public reading of the Scriptures; (6) public praise; and (7) the observing of the two sacraments (ordinances) of baptism and communion.[49] All of this should, of course, glorify God and edify His people.

Paul liked that word *edify*. He often used images from architecture to illustrate spiritual truths. Our English word *edify* comes from the Latin *aedificare*, "to build." The Greek word *(oikodomeō)* simply means "to build a house." The whole image goes back to our Lord's words, "I will build My church" (Matt. 16:18).

When Paul discussed the use and abuse of spiritual gifts (1 Cor. 14), one of his major points was the importance of edification in the church (14:3–5, 12, 17, 26). It was not enough that the worshiper *got* a blessing; he was supposed to *be* a blessing to others. He emphasized this same truth when he wrote to the Roman Christians who were dividing and disputing over special days and special diets. "Therefore let us pursue the things which make for peace and the things by which one may edify another" (Rom. 14:19).

The average worshiper probably does not realize the tensions that exist within a well-planned worship service. To begin with, there is a tension between the individual and the collective. We worship as individuals, but we are a part of the assembly; and we must neither lose our individuality nor cause others to lose theirs. Most people are content to be spectators, not participants; and sometimes those who do participate have a tendency to take over.

There is also a tension between the heritage of the past and the needs of the present. It is not enough merely to repeat an ancient ritual week by week or day by day; what we are doing must have a bearing on what we are experiencing right now. There is nothing wrong with ritual so long as it does not degenerate into *ritualism*. Ritual can beautifully preserve meaning and experience for us, or it can rob us of meaning and experience. If each new generation does not understand what is being said and done, the ceremonies accomplish nothing.

At the same time, we must beware of novelty, which is simply change for the sake of change. While the ultratraditional church is busy protecting its roots but not producing any fruits, the avant-garde congregations are cutting themselves free of their roots and becoming tumbleweeds that are "tossed to and fro and carried about with every wind of doctrine" (Eph. 4:14). Both extremes must be avoided.

Another difficult area of tension is the conflict between the objective and the subjective in worship. We are too prone to judge a worship experience by our feelings rather than by the fact that we obeyed God and tried to please and glorify Him. But most of the meals we eat are not spectacular gourmet productions, yet they nevertheless nourish us. If we think primarily of individual taste and not eternal truth, we may end up with an experience-centered service that ignores the past in order to gratify present appetites. People who run from church to church, searching for that "perfect worship experience," are impoverishing both themselves and the church—and they are chasing a religious mirage.

In other words, the true worshiper is really walking a knife's edge! He wants renewal but not novelty, personal enrichment but not at the expense of others, tradition but not empty ritualism, and objective truth that helps to produce a satisfying subjective experience. He will not enjoy this kind of creative balance every single time he attends worship, but at least he will have something to help him understand what is going on and be able to evaluate it honestly.

One of the greatest dangers is that we "use" worship in order to accomplish something else other than to glorify God in the edification of His church. We do not worship God in order to achieve peace of mind or to solve our personal problems, although these may be blessed by-products of worship. We worship God because He commands us to do so and because worship is the highest and holiest experience of the Christian believer. God is worthy of our worship, and that is all we really need to know. If our motive is anything other than this, then we are "using" God and practicing a refined form of idolatry.

Our "spiritual sacrifices" are given because He is worthy and not because they will "buy" us blessings. If our spiritual sacrifices become means to an end, they cease to be spiritual; and if they become ends in themselves, then our worship becomes empty ritual. It is not easy to maintain the balance and only the Spirit of God can enable us to do so.

"There is a use for ritual in a man's religious life," wrote the devotional writer Oswald Chambers. "When a man is in a right relationship to God ritual is an assistance; the place of worship and the atmosphere are both conducive to worship."[50]

A. W. Tozer wrote:

We of the non-liturgical churches tend to look with some disdain upon those churches that follow a carefully prescribed form of service, and certainly there must be a good deal in such services that has little or no meaning for the average participant—this not because it is carefully prescribed but because the average participant is what he is. But I have observed that our familiar impromptu service, planned by the leader twenty minutes before, often tends to follow a ragged and tired order. . . . The liturgical service is at least beautiful; ours is often ugly.[51]

WE EDIFY BY OUR PRESENCE

What kind of witness do we as believers bear to one another when we assemble to worship God? How do we help to transform one another by this witness?

To begin with, my very presence in a worship service says something positive to my fellow Christians. (Of course, they do not know my motive for being there, because only God sees the intents of the human heart.) My presence tells them that God is important in my life and that they are important to me as well. If I had stayed at home, I would not be able to "stir up love and good works" in the lives of others, nor would they be able to minister to me (Heb. 10:24).

When I was in the pastorate, my people often thanked me for my ministry each Sunday; but they were in turn ministering to me. In fact, I knew more about them and their needs than did perhaps any other member of the church. I knew that Mrs. Jenkins incurred the wrath of Mr. Jenkins when she came to church each Lord's Day, yet she was there and not complaining. (I think he let her come just so he could fuss about it all the rest of the day.) Her presence was an encouragement to me.

Mr. and Mrs. Keppler had to take turns attending church, so one of them could be at home caring for their afflicted son. "Grandma" Williams was in her usual place, even though getting out of bed and walking just a short distance to the church just about consumed her energy for the day, not to mention the pain she felt from her arthritis.

Jim Stewart worked the graveyard shift on weekends, so he just about had time to drive home from the mill, take a shower, gulp down breakfast, and then bring the family to Sunday school and church. If anybody had a good reason to stay home, it was Jim; but he was not only there, but he was serving in one ministry or another each Sunday. What this meant to his pastor, Jim can never know.

In other words, whenever one of God's children deliberately absents himself or herself from worship, that believer is saying to the rest of the family, "It really is not important to come to the Father's house to worship. The family can get along without you." Or, to change the image, the Christian soldier is saying to the rest of the troops, "It is perfectly acceptable to go AWOL! Sure, your place of duty is abandoned; but maybe the enemy won't notice."

Your very presence at worship is an affirmation of faith. You are letting others know that you take Matthew 6:33 seriously: "But seek first the kingdom of God and His righteousness, and all these things shall be added to you."

Have you ever made a list of the "one another" statements found in the New Testament? At least a dozen times, we are admonished to "love one another." Lest that important admonition be received in a vague fashion, it is fleshed out by a couple of dozen additional "one another" statements that further explain what Christian love really is. I am sure my list is not complete, but here are a few statements for you to consider:

Wash one another's feet—John 13:14
Prefer one another—Romans 12:10
Be of the same mind toward one another—Romans 12:16
Do not judge one another—Romans 14:13
Do not speak evil of one another—James 4:11
Edify one another—Romans 14:19; 1 Thessalonians 5:11
Receive one another—Romans 15:7
Admonish one another—Romans 15:14; Colossians 3:16
Care for one another—1 Corinthians 12:25
Minister gifts to one another—1 Peter 4:10
Greet one another—1 Corinthians 16:20
Serve one another—Galatians 5:13
Do not "bite and devour" one another—Galatians 5:15
Do not provoke one another—Galatians 5:26
Bear one another's burdens—Galatians 6:2
Forbear and forgive one another—Ephesians 4:32
Submit to one another—Ephesians 5:21; 1 Peter 5:5
Do not lie to one another—Ephesians 4:25; Colossians 3:9
Comfort one another—1 Thessalonians 4:18
Exhort one another—Hebrews 3:13
Consider one another—Hebrews 10:24
Do not grumble against one another—James 5:9
Confess your faults to one another—James 5:16
Pray for one another—James 5:16
Use hospitality one to another—1 Peter 4:9
Fellowship with one another—1 John 1:7

Of course, all of these ministries do not occur in each worship service, nor should they be limited to that time alone. The more we minister to one another in our daily lives, the easier it will be to minister to one another when we gather to worship God. What is important is that we have the "servant attitude" as we gather. We have not met "to be served, but to serve" (Matt. 20:28). We call our gathering a "service" because it is a time of serving: we minister to one another in the name of Jesus and to the glory of God. It is not only the "ministering staff" that shares in spiritual ministry; *every believer* has the privilege and responsibility of helping to edify others.

As I mentioned in an earlier chapter, I often see at the entrance of church buildings the words ENTER TO WORSHIP—DEPART TO SERVE, and I think I understand what they mean. However, it would be more biblical if the sign read: ENTER TO WORSHIP AND SERVE—AND DON'T QUIT WHEN YOU LEAVE THE BUILDING!

WE EDIFY BY OUR PARTICIPATION

The fact that the members of the body should minister and witness to one another indicates that our worship must include *participation*. What if there are believers who do not participate? Should their refusal to minister rob the rest of us of the blessing of being a blessing? I recall the frigid tones of a lady whom I personally invited to move in from the "fringes of the camp" and sit with the rest of the congregation at an evening service. "I have been sitting here for over twenty years," she informed me, "and I have no intentions of moving!" Poor soul! She was at the meeting, but she certainly was not in the fellowship of blessing.

I must confess that there was a time in my ministry when I wanted the worship services to be smooth productions that ran on schedule and presented no surprises. We on the platform would do the leading (led by the Lord, of course!), and the people in the pews would do the following. Participation? Well, that included singing the songs, entering into the spirit of the prayers, reading the proper responses from the back of the hymnal, praying for the preacher and, of course, putting something into the offering. God forbid that we should "interrupt" the worship of the Lord to hear a pressing prayer burden or the report of an exciting answer to prayer!

I must also confess that I resented the "noise" in the narthex (or, at Moody Church, the ambulatory) before the service, and the "noise" after the service *right in the sanctuary*. Didn't people know that we had assembled to worship God and not to chat with one another?

Now I realize that not only before and after our worship services, but also *during*, the saints need to minister to each other and bear witness of what God has done in their lives. To be sure, there must be order; but the order of a carefully planned worship service is enhanced, not destroyed, by the "interruptions" of the Spirit of God. Yes, we must watch out for the "evangelical exhibitionists" who want to show off; but let's not permit occasional nuisances to rob us all of ministries we can have to one another.

Each congregation must work out its own approach as the Spirit directs. All I am suggesting is that we see both the horizontal and the vertical relationships in worship. The word I need may not come from the pulpit. It may come from the fellow who meets me in the coat room and tells me what God did for him that previous week. Or I might meet a stranger in the parking lot and discover God has a word for him from me.

I realize that the larger the congregation, the more difficult it is to invite and enjoy participation. But usually larger churches have adequate public address systems so that a witnessing believer could be heard by the rest of the congregation. For that matter, why not invite the witnesses to the platform? Certainly some spiritual leader in the church must screen these participants in advance lest some stranger create problems, but this ought not to be much of a task. I know from experience that large congregations attract "strange people" who like to be noticed, but large congregations also attract burdened people who desperately need to hear what God can do in the lives of people *other than the platform personnel*.

As long as I am confessing my sins, I might as well mention that my mind has changed about "greeting one another" at some point in the meeting. I used to resist this practice with a holy passion. Perhaps it was an overreaction caused by my Youth for Christ days when we always shook hands and sang "Heavenly Sunshine." Too often in church services, the timing has been wrong—the result of poor planning—so that when I should have been bowed in submissive adoration, I was instead having my hand pumped by a fellow from Dubuque who had read one of my books and was pleased to meet me.

But whatever abuses we may cultivate in this particular practice,

I believe we do more damage by omitting the practice completely. After all, the members of the early church did receive one another and they were admonished to "greet one another"—and even "with a holy kiss"! (Check 1 Cor. 16:20; 2 Cor. 13:12; Rom. 16:16; 1 Thess. 5:26; 1 Pet. 5:14.) While I certainly would not recommend indiscriminate and promiscuous kissing that reflected more of the erotic than the spiritual, I think that believers do need to greet one another and give some evidence of affection and appreciation. J. B. Phillips translated the phrase, "a handshake all around, please!" and perhaps he has the right idea.

Church historians tell us that the "holy kiss" was given to newly baptized people, backsliders who had repented and been restored to fellowship (see Luke 15:20), and also to candidates for ordination. Some historians include the "kiss of peace" at the agape supper and the Lord's Supper. People often kissed when they met (Luke 7:45) and when they parted (Acts 20:37). When Judas kissed the Lord Jesus, he did what every disciple did when he met his master. Of course, in Judas's case, the kiss was a vile act of treachery.

Perhaps each church must solve the problem locally of how to "pass the peace" or "share the love" among the members of the congregation. Not everybody has the kind of effusive personality that openly demonstrates love—and some who do demonstrate it with enthusiasm may occasionally go to extremes. So be it. Better that our fellowship should be criticized for being *too* friendly than not friendly at all.

WE EDIFY BY OUR SONG AND SPEECH

We witness to others not only by our presence and our personal greeting, however it may be expressed, but also by what we say and sing and the way we do it. When we sing, we are not only worshiping the Lord, but we are also "speaking to one another in psalms and hymns and spiritual songs" (Eph. 5:19). The choir and soloists are not the only ones who witness through song; each member of the congregation also bears witness even though individual voices may not be distinguished. The witness is there.

On many occasions, congregational singing has ministered to me and helped to carry me through a difficult time. Old familiar songs have suddenly become "new s[...] [...] through the congregation. And w[...] [...] also helps to educate the saints, pro[...] cal. "One generation shall praise Yo[...] declare Your mighty acts" (Ps. 145:4). [...] he shall praise You, as I do this day; the fa[...] truth to the children" (Isa. 38:19).

I will have more to say about Christian m[...] but I do want to emphasize this personal conv[...] more right to sing a lie than a preacher has to p[...] et our singing be theologically sound as well as technic[...] quate. No amount of beautiful harmony can atone for theologi[...] heresy.

Of course, singing is not the only vocal witness that we may give. We may also give a testimony of what God has said to us or done for us. We may feel led to quote a passage from God's Word or perhaps stand up and read it. The contribution of witness that we give in the assembly will pretty much be determined by our personal walk with the Lord day by day. True witness is not manufactured; it flows creatively from within. "Keep your heart with all diligence, for out of it spring the issues of life" (Prov. 4:23).

Not every believer is led by God at every service to bear witness to every blessing God has given him, but each of us should be sensitive to God's direction. Sometimes the Lord brings together two or three witnesses whose words blend in a remarkable way and together convey a precious truth for the church to receive and apply. I do not believe that God is giving us new revelations today, for we have His completed revelation in the Word. However, He desires to share with His people new insights into His truth, spiritual illumination that enables us to see our situation in the light of His revelation. The old Puritan John Robinson was right when he wrote, "Fresh light yet shall break out of God's Word."

WE EDIFY BY OBSERVING THE LORD'S SUPPER

When the church observes the ordinances or sacraments, it has a marvelous opportunity to bear witness and to remind God's people of what the Savior did for them. It is unfortunate that both baptism and Communion have been used by some believers for dispute and divi[...]

...ing new: Paul had to deal with the same problem ...fronted the church at Corinth. "Is Christ divided?" he ...em. "Was Paul crucified for you? Or were you baptized in the ...me of Paul?" (1 Cor. 1:13). "For by one Spirit we were all baptized into one body—whether Jews or Greeks, whether slaves or free—and have all been made to drink into one Spirit" (12:13).

We need to be reminded regularly of our Lord's death, burial, resurrection, and coming again, and of the presence and ministry of the Holy Spirit in the church. These precious truths should come back to us whenever we witness a baptism or participate in the Communion service. As we reflect on them, we certainly ought to love Him more and want to promote the unity and purity of His church.

I want to focus primarily on the Lord's Supper—or Communion, or Eucharist—because our participation is definitely an act of worship and witness. It is here that the church meets at the table as a family, just as the Jewish families met around the table to celebrate the first Passover feast (see Exod. 12). No stranger was allowed to share in the meal, and all who shared were "under the blood" and protected from the promised judgment.

If our observance of the Lord's Supper is to be an act of worship and witness, there are certain facts that we must keep in mind and certain responsibilities we must fulfill.

To begin with, the Communion or Eucharist is *a meal*, and we have the responsibility of *receiving*. Our Lord took some of the elements of the Passover feast, bread and wine in particular, and enriched them with new spiritual meaning. Bread and wine were common elements, present on every table for every meal. It was just like our Lord to take the ordinary things and touch them with glory, for with Him there was no "secular" or "sacred." "Therefore, whether you eat or drink, or whatever you do, do all to the glory of God" (1 Cor. 10:31).

When we receive the bread and the cup, we are bearing witness that we have first of all received the true Bread of Life into our very being, and that we have trusted the Savior Who shed His blood for us. Leon Morris explains it well: "Those who do not eat and drink have no life. Eating and drinking thus appear to be a very graphic way of saying that men must take Christ into their innermost being."[52]

The Communion is not only a meal, but is a *memorial* meal and we

have the responsibility of *remembe*...
ing of the Communion, twice he ha...
of Me" (1 Cor. 11:24, 25). But the w...
(anamnēsis) means much more than r...
someone from the past. Jesus is alive, and...
His passion are with us today. We "remem...
and our hearts as we, through the Spirit, ...
with the Lord. We *were* redeemed, but we also...
shall be redeemed fully when He returns ("til... or.
11:26). We are not simply remembering an event, ... ecover
an emotion; we are realizing an experience as we fi... hearts and
minds on the Savior.

It is also a *family* meal, and we have the responsibility of *relating*.
Judas, the unbeliever, was not present when Jesus instituted the Communion. The men who were present were far from perfect, and even
sinned right there at the table by arguing over who was the greatest;
but they were all believers and therefore redeemed by Christ. They
did not come to the table to be redeemed; they came to the table because they already were redeemed. They were "His own" (John
13:1), His "little children" (v. 33) whom He had cleansed
(vv. 10, 11).

As we participate in the Lord's Supper, we are bearing witness to
the unity of the family of God. "For we, though many, are one bread
and one body; for we all partake of that one bread" (1 Cor. 10:17). As
we participate, it must be with a recognition that we are a part of
God's wonderful family in heaven and on earth. Paul called this "discerning the Lord's body" (11:29). We meet *at a table*, where there is
unity and equality before the Lord. We are one in Jesus Christ.

During the preaching of the Word, the minister is usually elevated above the congregation; but when we assemble for the Communion, we are all on the same level. It has well been said, "The ground
is level at the foot of the cross." To use the Table of the Lord in a
divisive manner to promote sectarianism is to destroy one of the precious messages that the Supper declares.

Finally, the Communion is a *victorious meal*. We do not come
together to remember our sins, but to rejoice in our Savior and the
victory He has won for us. "And I bestow upon you a kingdom," the
Master told His disciples, "just as My Father bestowed one upon Me,

...nd drink at My table in My kingdom, and sit on
...g the twelve tribes of Israel" (Luke 22:29, 30). What a
...ation of victory!

At the Table, we look back and recall the events of His passion;
we look within and "remember" so that we may experience the blessings of that sacrifice today; and we look ahead, knowing that He shall
come again and receive us into His eternal kingdom. What a cause for
celebration! And the fact that all of God's people, regardless of denominational label, will be together in heaven ought to encourage us
to practice and promote true spiritual unity today (John 17:20–24).

True worship involves witness, to God, to one another, and to a
lost world. That will be our next consideration.

GRACIOUS FATHER,

*I confess that often I have not witnessed to my fellow believers. I have tried
to worship You, but I have not tried to edify others.*

Forgive me..

Help me to see that I cannot claim to love You if I fail to love my brother.

*Deliver me from becoming a "spiritual snob" who thinks he can get along
without the help of his brothers and sisters in Christ. By my presence, my
actions, and my words, help me to bear witness to them and encourage them
in the faith. At the Table, help me to remember the Savior and discern the
body.*

*Father, too often in the worship service, I have only looked up. Please help
me to look around. I may discover You in the smile or handshake of a
brother or sister in Christ.*

In His Name,
AMEN.

CHAPTER 11 *In which we learn that preaching is an act of worship*

IN THE PREACHING of God's Word, the church witnesses both to itself and to a lost world, but this is true *only* if the preaching is truly an act of worship. If preaching is not an act of worship then the church will end up worshiping the preacher and what he says rather than worshiping God. "When I declare the Word of God I offer sacrifice," said Martin Luther. "When thou hearest the Word of God with all thy heart, thou dost offer sacrifice."

Whenever you hear someone talking about "the preliminaries" of the service as opposed to "the preaching of the Word," you know that he or she does not look upon preaching as an act of worship. "Preaching, if not sacramental, is profane," write R. J. Coates and J. I. Packer. "By this we mean that a true sermon is an act of God, and not a mere performance by man. In real preaching the speaker is the servant of the word and God speaks and works by the word through his servant's lips."[3] The witness to God, the witness to the church, and the witness to a lost world are all brought together in the proclamation of the Word.

I recall the first time I preached in a church that had a divided chancel. I was accustomed to seeing the pulpit central and elevated, with the communion table before it on a lower level. After all, God worked through the preaching of His Word! I have since discovered that the arrangement of the furniture is not necessarily an indication of the church's orthodoxy or lack of it.

For that matter, it is unfortunate that some well-meaning people, orthodox and otherwise, have kept alive this untenable idea of prophetic ministry *versus* priestly ministry, as though the two are mutually exclusive and competitive. Jeremiah, Ezekiel, and John the Baptist were all from priestly families, yet they were called to prophetic ministry. At the Lord's Table, we "proclaim the Lord's death till He comes" (1 Cor. 11:26); and the Greek word translated "proclaim" is translated "preach" at least six times in Acts. To quote Coates and Packer again, "The sacraments serve the word; they minister blessing precisely by the ministry of the word."[4]

Paul looked upon his ministry of the gospel as a "priestly ministry." Paul used the word *latreuō* ("the priestly service of God") in Romans 1:9 to describe his ministry of the gospel; and in Romans 15:16, he used *leitourgos* which gives us our English word *liturgy*. Both words have priestly overtones: Paul saw his evangelistic ministry as that of a priest, bringing the people won to Christ as sacrifices on the altar, to the glory of God. He saw himself as "a minister [*leitourgos*] of Jesus Christ to the Gentiles, ministering [*hierourgeō*, ministering as a priest] the gospel of God, that the offering [*prosphora*, a sacrificial offering] of the Gentiles might be acceptable, sanctified by the Holy Spirit" (Rom. 15:16). What a high and holy view, not only of preaching, but also of personal evangelism!

When you look upon preaching and evangelism as acts of spiritual worship, it certainly makes a difference in your ministry. For one thing, it helps to purify your motives. The minister who preaches or who seeks to win the lost simply because this is God's commandment is going to operate from a feeling of guilt; and this is not the highest motive for service. Preachers who feel guilty have a tendency to want to make their listeners feel guilty, and we do not go to a worship service to be indicted. The preacher is a witness, not a prosecuting attorney, and if he reveals God to us in the Word, there will be plenty of opportunity for the Spirit to convict us. Isaiah saw the glory of God and was only too willing to confess his sins.

If preaching is an act of worship, then the preacher must not present to God that which has cost him nothing (2 Sam. 24:24). Malachi reprimanded the priests of his day because they were not giving God their best. They put defiled food on God's altar and brought sacrifices that were lame and sick (Mal. 1:6-8). Before we criticize them too severely, we had better examine our own "spiritual sacrifices," particularly our sermons.

THE PROBLEM OF ACADEMIC PREACHING

"Great heights of adoration, praise, and worship can be reached by a devout congregation during the sermon, as the things of God pass before them."⁵⁵ Alas, too often the sermon does not "proclaim the praises" of the Lord (1 Pet. 2:9, literal translation)! Instead of seeing the Lord, we see the preacher. Or we see an outline as the sanctuary is changed into a lecture room, sometimes with the aid of an overhead projector. The emphasis is on content and "teaching," which certainly is commendable; but there is much more to preaching than passing along religious information. It must reveal, not mere facts about God, but the Person of God Himself.

If the experience of the Emmaus disciples is a pattern for believers today, then the blessing of true Bible exposition is an ignited heart, not an inflated head. "Did not our heart burn within us while He talked with us on the road, and while He opened the Scriptures to us?" (Luke 24:32). The Corinthians were proud of their spiritual knowledge, but they lacked love; so Paul reminded them, "Knowledge puffs up, but loves edifies" (1 Cor. 8:1). And he reminded Timothy, "Now the purpose of the commandment is love from a pure heart, from a good conscience, and from sincere faith" (1 Tim. 1:5).

Because we have lost this high view of preaching as an act of worship, we are now suffering the consequences both in our worship services and in our preaching. Preaching is not what it ought to be and neither is worship. What God has joined together, we have put asunder, and we are paying for it.

For one thing, much preaching today is very academic. We think we have to explain everything and outline everything. I do not agree with his theology, but Harry Emerson Fosdick was right when he said that the purpose of preaching was not to explain a subject but to achieve an object. We are so wrapped up today in the *content* that we have forgotten the *intent*. As I said before, we have turned the sanctuary into a lecture room. The most important thing about a sermon is not what God writes on our hearts as we see Him in the Word, but what we write in our notebooks!

An outline is not a message from God any more than a recipe is a meal or a blueprint is a building. "It is possible for a man to analyse the Bible and lose it in the process," said G. Campbell Morgan, himself a great expositor; "to prepare a synthesis of the Bible and lose his soul at the work; to make himself perfectly familiar with the letter, and to find out that the letter killeth because he has lost touch with the spirit."[56]

How easy it is for the preacher to perfect a homiletical technique that enables him to manufacture sermons week after week. If he is really good at all, his listeners will comment on his outlines but rarely confess that what he said helped them to see God and worship Him. For the most part, listening to a sermon is an intellectual experience rather than the worship experience of the total person. When preaching is an act of worship, the listener's heart is stirred by the vision of God and the Spirit of God says far more to him than what the minister declares from the pulpit. When preaching is an act of worship, the outline is to the text what a prism is to a shaft of sunlight: it breaks it up so that its beauty and wonder are clearly seen.

We not only have a tendency to analyze everything to death (and I am as guilty as anyone else!), but we also feel compelled to explain everything and leave out the mystery that must always belong to God. Since true worship involves wonder, there must always be some degree of mystery. When Paul completed his section in Romans on the sovereignty of God, he did not write, "There! I have explained everything!" Rather, as we have noted in a previous chapter, he moved from writing to worshiping, from theology to doxology, and he wrote, "Oh, the depth of the riches both of the wisdom and knowledge of God! How unsearchable are His judgments and His ways past finding out!" (Rom. 11:33). Though he was an inspired apostle who had gone to heaven and come back, Paul did not feel compelled to explain everything. He left room for mystery.

The rustic preacher who said "Some things are better felt than telt" had poor grammar but excellent philosophy. The Bible is written for the heart as well as the head; otherwise it would not be saturated as it is with poetry, symbolism, and just about every literary device that captures the imagination and the emotions. After all, preaching deals with real life, the life in the Word and the life in the pew; and it takes imagination to build that bridge from an ancient book to a modern need. Northrop Frye defined imagination as "the power of constructing possible models of human experience."[57] When Jesus wanted to help people stop worrying, He did not give a lecture on Hebrew and Greek words. Instead, He talked about birds, flowers, and robbers. He appealed to the imagination of His listeners, gripped their hearts, and then instructed their minds.

THE PREACHER AS GOD'S MESSENGER

I am certainly not suggesting that the minister ignore the fundamentals of hermeneutics and homiletics; nor am I suggesting that poor outlines and careless presentations of the Word are marks of a spiritual ministry. I am only saying that it is easy for preachers to get so wrapped up in their outlines that they forget their message from God. If preaching is not an act of worship, the preacher can easily make an idol of the outline. The purpose of preaching is not to inform the congregation of the minister's homiletical gifts; it is to bring the congregation face to face with the living God.

When Campbell Morgan was a young preacher in Rugeley, he was already in demand for preaching missions. People were beginning to notice that Morgan was a gifted expositor, and Morgan was beginning to notice it too. One Sunday, after a particularly successful evening service, Morgan sat in his study alone, pondering his life and ministry. God's voice seemed to say to him, "What are you going to be, a preacher, or My messenger?"

All that night he wrestled with himself and with God. When the dawn came, Morgan had surrendered. "Thy messenger, my Master—Thine!" he cried out. Then he took a bundle of outlines of his popular sermons and threw it into the fireplace. That was when the victory was completely won. "The work of many years was destroyed on that golden morning," said Morgan, "when I stepped out to follow God at all costs, determining to do so without those sermons."[58]

A minister need not be especially gifted or famous to face this kind of crisis. (Perhaps most of us should burn our sermon outlines *before* we preach them!) When the sermon becomes an end in itself instead of a means to the end, then we are confronted with idolatry. When preaching is an act of worship and the message is given to God as an offering from the minister's heart, then God can take the message and bless it.

When I was senior minister at the Moody Church, I did my best to protect my Saturday evenings. During the week, I had prepared my messages; but on Saturday evenings, I had to take time to prepare myself. I used to go into my little study at home, look over my messages in the light of that week's pastoral work, and make whatever changes I thought would improve them. Then, I would pick up each outline and hold it before the Lord, presenting it as a sacrifice to Him.

"Father," I would say, "here is the message I plan to deliver tomorrow. I present it to You as a sacrifice. It has cost me in time, study, and prayer; and I do not want to give You anything that has cost me nothing. Please accept this message as my gift to You. Help me to preach it as an act of worship. May You be glorified in it all."

On more than one Saturday evening, I had to confess that the previous week had been hectic, study time had been at a premium, and my message was not all that I wanted it to be. But it was the best I could do, and I presented it to the Lord in that light. How many times His mercy was granted! How many times He ignited the little offering that I put on His altar and gave us a season of spiritual heat and light! I wish I had learned earlier in my ministry that preaching must be an act of worship if the message is to help people and glorify God.

Consider these words from Frank Cairns, spoken during his Warrack Lectures in 1934:

Gentlemen, if you are ever to serve God by your preaching, you have got to make up your mind as to whether it has or has not the right to be regarded as an essential part of the worship of God; you must have a clear idea as to whether your preaching is for you an act of worship—an offering to God which you can make with a clear conscience, and a wholehearted devotion, and a humble faith, or whether it is something which—be it either cheap or tawdry, or manifesting both erudition and literary skill—could not be regarded as possessing the authority of the Word of God or any Divine Sanction whatsoever, and which might as well be tied in a napkin and buried in the earth for all the value it has for the purpose of bringing the human soul face to face with God.[59]

THE IMPACT OF PREACHING AS WORSHIP

When preaching is an act of worship, there is (for lack of a better term) an *immediacy* to the impact of the Word. In this day of cassette recorders, I fear that too many worshipers deliberately delay their hearing of the Word until a more convenient season. Or, if the worshiper is the kind of person who takes notes, he or she may be so intent on writing down the outline and choice statements that the immediate impact of the message is lost. And, if the preacher has a literary bent, his sermons may be prepared with the publishers in mind and not the worshipers.

I may be wrong, but I believe that God wants to speak to us immediately and do something toward the transforming of our lives. This is not to deny that a message may be used by the Spirit weeks after the service has ended. It is only to affirm that when preaching is an act of worship, and listening to preaching is an act of worship, people see and hear God and there is an immediate impact on their hearts and minds. When the sermon is an academic lecture, no response is required except "I agree" or "I disagree." But when a sermon is presented as an integral part of Christian worship, the listener must do something about the revelation of God that the Spirit brings to him.

"What can be more truly described as worship," asked the theologian-preacher James Denney, "than hearing the Word of God as it ought to be heard, hearing it with penitence, with contrition, with faith and self-consecration, with vows of new obedience? If this is not worship in spirit and in truth, what is?"[60] Instead, the usual response is, "Fine message, Pastor!" which means, being interpreted, "I got the outline and learned something new from the Bible. The hour was not wasted!"

While reading Psalm 119 during my regular devotional time, I could not help but notice that the psalmist combined prayer, praise and Bible study. "I will praise You with uprightness of heart, when I learn Your righteous judgments" (v. 7). "Blessed are You, O LORD [praise]! Teach me Your statutes [prayer and learning]" (v. 12). "Accept, I pray, the freewill offerings of my mouth, O LORD, and teach me Your judgments" (v. 108). "My lips shall utter praise, for You teach me Your statutes" (v. 171).

In other words, there is no conflict between praise and preaching *if* preaching is an act of worship. When the man or woman in the pew closes the hymnal and opens the Bible, there is no jarring note, nor is it necessary for them to "shift gears" either mentally or emotionally. From the beginning of the service to the end, our eyes are open to God's glory and our ears to God's truth. There are no "preliminaries" to be "gotten out of the way."

Finally, when preaching is an act of worship, the Word is applied personally to our lives. Academic outlines prepared by a minister who has not seen God as the material was prepared, will never transform the lives of the listeners. "There is scarcely anything so dull and meaningless as Bible doctrine taught for its own sake," wrote A. W. Tozer in his penetrating essay "Exposition Must Have Application." "Truth divorced from life is not truth in its Biblical sense, but something else and something less. . . . Truth engages the citadel of the human heart and is not satisfied until it has conquered everything there. The will must come forth and surrender its sword. It must stand at attention to receive orders, and those orders it must joyfully obey. Short of this any knowledge of Christian truth is inadequate and unavailing."[61]

The purpose of the Word of God is to reveal the God of the Word; and when you meet the God of the Word, you must do something about His will. As we saw in an earlier chapter, the people in Scripture who saw God were never quite the same again. Their lives had been transformed. Unless the minister sees God as he prepares the message, the listeners are not likely to see Him. To quote Tozer again: "The scribes who sat in Moses' seat were not the victims of error; they were the victims of their failure to experience the truth they taught."[62]

The kind of preaching the unsaved world needs to hear is not manufactured from books, although serious study is certainly necessary. You do not "build a sermon" by borrowing pieces from Spurgeon, Billy Sunday, the morning newspaper, and the notes in your study Bible. A message from God is the living consequence of a vital meeting with God during which you worshiped Him and permitted His truth to set fire to your soul. When the minister's study turns into a sanctuary, a holy of holies, then something transforming will happen as the Word of God is proclaimed. As our lives are transformed, the church will be transformed; and this will open the way for us to reach out to a lost world that knows not God. Then we will see come to pass what Paul wrote to the Corinthians: "And thus the secret of his [the unsaved visitor's] heart are revealed; and so, falling down on his face, he will worship God and report that God is truly among you" (1 Cor. 14:25).

FATHER,

I know You have forgiven me for my sins. But can You ever forgive me for my sermons?

Forgive me for being clever, for presenting Your truth in neat human packages that robbed You of glory.

Forgive me for preaching to impress rather than to express. Forgive me for predictable preaching that lacked surprises and heavenly interruptions.

Help me to so open the Word that hearts will burn and people will say, "We have seen the Lord!" May each message be fresh from the altar, fragrant with heavenly incense and ignited by divine fire.

Remind me, O Lord, of the awesomeness of preaching. Convict me when I find it easy to manufacture outlines and feed my people on substitutes.

Apart from You, Lord, I can do nothing. With You, I can do all things.

I don't want to be a preacher only. Please, make me Your messenger.

Whatever it is that I must burn—here are the ashes.

Reveal Yourself to me, and help me to reveal You to others as I proclaim Your Word.

In Jesus' Name,
AMEN.

CHAPTER 12 *In which we try to relate worship and the arts, trusting to enrich both*

MARTIN LUTHER IS reported to have said that God gave us five senses with which to worship Him and that it would be sheer ingratitude for us to use less.[63] God has also given us a beautiful world to live in, a world filled with beautiful things that can be used to glorify Him. After all, our God is a God of beauty. Our world may be travailing in pain because of Adam's fall, but it is still declaring the glory of God and revealing day and night His wisdom and power.

Even atheistic and agnostic scholars admit that some of the greatest art, literature, and music have had their inspiration from the Scriptures, especially the Gospel story. The believer with his or her knowledge of the Bible ought to appreciate these great artistic achievements all the more; but, alas, too often they do not. Believers want architectural beauty in their homes but not in the church building. They want wedding ceremonies to be beautiful, complete with lighted candles and classical music; but the morning worship service can be planned at the last minute—and don't you dare use candles!

There is a strange attitude in the evangelical world that moves people almost to delight in opposing and even destroying the beautiful and the artistic. This attitude is born of a false dichotomy that is unbiblical in its divorcing of "matter" and "spirit." The advocates of this approach tell us that God is concerned with the soul and not the body, and that the spiritual is far more important than the material.

This philosophy is destroyed by one great event: the Incarnation. If matter is evil, or is not important, why did God become man? If we are to focus only on the invisible, why did God become visible? "The Lordship of Christ over the whole of life," wrote Francis Schaeffer, "means that there are no platonic areas in Christianity, no dichotomy or hierarchy between the body and the soul."[64] A beautiful building or statue or song can glorify God and bear witness to Him just as much as a devout prayer or a fine sermon.

We are wrestling, of course, with the problem of the relationship between religion and the arts. Every believer must deal with this issue, whether his or her worship experience is in a plain hall above a grocery store or a towering cathedral at the heart of a city. What is the legitimate use of the arts in Christian worship?

John Calvin wrote that "because sculpture and painting are gifts of God, I seek a pure and legitimate use of each, lest those things which the Lord has conferred upon us for his glory and our good be not only polluted by perverse misuse but also turned to our destruction."[65]

While Calvin may not totally agree with me, I believe that worship needs the arts and the arts need worship. Over the centuries the arts have certainly been used to attack the church when they should have been used by the church to attack the enemy. David was wise enough to take Goliath's sword and use it in his battles.

It was Calvin's view that "only those things are to be sculptured or painted which the eyes are capable of seeing"[66] and this eliminates God, the angels, and the past events of history (although he admitted that such historical paintings might have "some use in teaching or admonition"). Calvin appears to have had a pragmatic view of art: its main purpose was to glorify God and teach His people.

Luther, as usual, was much more outspoken. "I am not of the opinion that arts are to be cast down and destroyed on account of the Gospel, as some fanatics protest; on the other hand I would gladly see all arts, especially music, in the service of Him who has given and created them."[67]

If we do not use the creative arts, then religion becomes an abstraction that is expressed and explained in words only. We use the arts in every other area of human life—why should we exclude our faith? Why live only with abstractions?

The danger, of course, is that of idolatry. The Hebrew nation was only too conscious of God's unequivocal declaration in the first and second commandments (Exod. 20:1-6). But God did put beauty within the tabernacle and the temple (see 2 Chron. 3:6), and He inspired David to organize the singers, write songs for them, and even design musical instruments (1 Chron. 23:1-6).

As I mentioned before, it is the incarnation of Jesus Christ that seals our mandate for using the concrete in order to reveal the abstract and the invisible. God came to us in human flesh. He entered into the everyday experiences of life. He sanctified bread and wine. He saw God in the lilies and the birds. He used parables, metaphors, and similes to convey profound truths. He appealed to the sanctified imagination of His disciples who, too often, were such literalists that they completely missed His meaning (note John 2:19-22; 4:31-34; 11:11-13). In every way, our Lord encourages us to use art forms in the service of the gospel.

It is beyond the scope of this book to deal with the many difficult questions that this subject presents to us, but some of these questions we cannot avoid.

THE NATURE OF ART

To begin with, what is art? A critic of another generation, Irwin Edman, wrote that "art is the name for that whole process of intelligence which life, understanding its own conditions, turns them [statues, pictures, and symphonies] to the most interesting or exquisite account."[68] The Christian artist receives what he has as the gift of God and creates what he does to the glory of God. He sees himself as a steward, as one sharing with God in the miracle of creativity. We are told that Johann Sebastian Bach often put the letters *S D G* on his compositions, signifying *Soli Deo Gloria*, "to God alone be the glory."

Two experiences my wife and I had in England come to mind, both of them from our first visit. We had just finished touring St. Paul's Cathedral and were quite impressed with what we saw. But it was so unlike our churches at home! Where were the meetings held? Could the people ever hear a sermon here? When our guide asked for questions, my wife asked, "Why was this building built?" Without pausing, the guide replied, "Why, to the glory of God!"

Westminster Abbey was the location for the second experience. I had noticed some damage in a lovely carved screen, so I asked the guide what caused it. She stiffened up like a soldier on duty, pursed her lips, and said, "Why the Puritans tried to wreck it! They tried to wreck everything!"

The way we evaluate beauty, its place and its use, can be an evidence of what we believe about God and His creation. It is true that the Puritans were plain people who opposed anything that smacked of papal idolatry, including lovely altar screens. That they carried their iconoclastic crusades too far is probably true, just as it is true that the established church of their day probably carried their nonevangelical embellishments too far.

If art is our master, then it becomes idolatry; but if art is our servant, it becomes ministry. Anything symbolic, from a communion wafer to a cathedral, can become an idol if we permit. But the minute it becomes an idol, it loses the power to encourage spiritual life and growth. God does not live in buildings or wafers, but He can make use of both to reveal Himself to us. The experience of the worshiper does not stop at the bread in his hand or the building around him; it goes beyond and reaches to God. True art is simply man's attempt to use what God gives him to touch our senses so that experience (religious or otherwise) is clarified and interpreted.

"But all we need is the Bible!" the opposition declares. "What need have we for poetry, symbols, and so forth? Let God be God and let Him be seen in His Word!"

That is a noble declaration of faith in the importance of the Bible; but it is not too intelligent, because the Bible itself is made up of "poetry, symbols, and so forth." The Bible is a work of art, inspired by the Spirit of God. In it God uses narrative, poems, riddles, similes and metaphors, parables, symbols and other literary devices to convey His truth to us. Jesus did not give a lecture on hermeneutics; He simply said, "The seed is the word of God." Paul did not try to explain all the intricate relationships between Jesus Christ and His church; instead, he compared Christ to a bridegroom and the church to a bride. The capstone of the Bible, the book of Revelation, is saturated with religious symbolism, related no doubt to Daniel and Ezekiel.

To defend the Bible, then, is to defend the right use of the arts to convey the message of God's truth.

THE FUNCTION OF ART

But what is art supposed to accomplish? It is simply supposed to imitate nature—or is there more involved? Calvin admitted that the arts could be useful in instructing people, and this would be especially true where illiteracy might abound. The stained-glass windows of the medieval cathedrals were used to teach many an uneducated peasant the basic stories of the Bible. Likewise, the miracle plays dramatized doctrine and taught the crowds far more than they were likely to learn from their dull preachers.

But Christian art must be more than imitation and instruction; it must also be interpretation. The artist sees and senses reality and then tries to convey that experience to us in a poem, a play, a song, a picture. When I was in my first pastorate, we built a new church sanctuary, and the designing of it was quite an experience for me. Of course, like most neighborhood churches, we had to watch the budget; and I suggested to the architect that we build a simple square building, but put a "church façade" at the front to make it look better.

He looked at me, shook his head, and said, "Young man, we are designing a church. There should be nothing fake about a church building! A façade is a form of deception, and we want no deception in a church!"

Our architect would have gotten along beautifully with Charles Spurgeon, for that great preacher believed that art was very definitely an expression of theology. When his great tabernacle in London was being designed, Spurgeon made it clear that the building would be Grecian and not Gothic. "We owe nothing to the Goths as religionists," he explained. "We have a great part of our Scriptures in the Grecian language, and this shall be a Grecian place of worship; and God give us the power and life of that master of the Grecian tongue, the apostle Paul, that here like wonders may be done by the preaching of the Word as were wrought by his ministry!"[69]

The Christian artist must be an interpreter who helps us to see and understand experience. He is not manufacturing mirrors that merely reflect what we already see; he is giving us windows through which we may see what we have never seen. He is also giving us doors that open out into new experiences. Idolatry is a limiting thing that draws narrow boundaries. True artistry is a liberating thing that points out horizons and dares us to launch out into the deep.

This is the way Irwin Edman explains it:

The artist when he ceases to be merely a gifted and trifling craftsman turns out to be, in his very choice of themes, in his selection of materials, in his total and residual effect, a commentator on life and existence; in his immediate and imaginative way he is a philosopher.[70]

This is why we had better be careful which artists we select for the creative works that go into the worship of the Lord.

MUSIC

Let's think about Christian music and its relationship to art and worship. "The world was born to the sound of music," writes Richard Allen Bodey. "At its creation 'the morning stars sang together, and all the sons of God shouted for joy' (Job 38:7). On the night the Savior of the world was born, a thunderous doxology sung by angel choirs, 'Glory to God in the highest' (Luke 2:14), burst over the Judean hills and echoed across the arches of the heavens."[71] If a person wants to participate in Christian worship, he or she will have a difficult time escaping singing.

The first music mentioned in the Bible is connected with the civilization of Cain who had turned his back on God. Jubal was "the father of all those who play the harp and flute" (Gen. 4:21). His name, by the way, gives us our English word *jubilee,* and the Hebrew word means "a trumpet or ram's horn." The fact that music seems to have originated with the God-rejecting Cainites has led some believers to reject (or at least suspect) the use of instrumental music in Christian worship. It is acceptable to sing the Psalms, but always without accompaniment. The Brethren writer C. H. Macintosh wrote:

> As in Cain's day, the grateful sounds of "the harp and organ," no doubt, completely drowned, to man's ear, the cry of Abel's blood; so now, man's ear is filled with other sounds than those which issue from Calvary, and his eye filled with other objects than a crucified Christ.[72]

The author seems to be suggesting that sounds for the ear and sights for the eye can bring ruin to the soul, and indeed they may; but we need to remember that God had beauty in both sound and sight long before Cain's descendants went to work. In his commentary on Genesis 4:22, Calvin admitted that "the liberal arts and sciences have descended to us from the heathen." But he did not believe that this fact should rob us of the privilege of using the arts and sciences for the glory of God.

> Now, although the invention of the harp, and of similar instruments of music, may minister to our pleasure, rather than to our necessity, still it is not to be thought altogether superfluous; much less does it deserve, in itself, to be condemned. . . . But such is the nature of music, that it can be adapted to the offices of religion, and made profitable to men; if only it be free from vicious attractions, and from the foolish delight, by which it seduces men from better employments, and occupies them in vanity.[73]

Once again, Luther pulls no punches. "Music is God's greatest gift. It has often so stimulated and stirred me that I felt the desire to preach."[74] He also said, "I place music next to theology and give it the highest praise."[75] Luther was himself an excellent musician and led the way toward restoring scriptural songs and congregational singing to the worship services.

The young pastor learns early that "music is the War Department of the church." A veteran minister said to me, "I think when Satan fell, he landed in the choir loft." To be fair all around, we must admit that there are times when Satan may have landed in the pulpit!

Music is important to God's people. It is one of our best ways of expressing praise to God, and it is an effective means of education and evangelism. We witness to God, to the church, and to the lost world whenever we sing. Music is also a means of strengthening and expressing unity in the church. Except for the song books published by cultic religious groups, the Christian hymnal is a beautiful example of true biblical ecumenicity. A Baptist congregation will enthusiastically sing songs by a Methodist ("Christ the Lord is Risen Today!"), an Anglican ("Rock of Ages, Cleft for Me"), and even a Roman Catholic ("Jesus, the Very Thought of Thee"). People who dislike classical music will sing melodies borrowed from Beethoven ("Joyful, Joyful We Adore Thee") and Haydn ("Glorious Things of Thee are Spoken"). Music is a universal language, to be sure.

Why is it that music creates so much conflict among the people of God? For one thing, music confronts the whole person—mind, heart, and will—and demands some kind of response. Music instructs the mind, inspires the emotions, and challenges the will. Boswell admitted to Samuel Johnson that music influenced him strongly. "I told him that it affected me to such a degree, as often to agitate my nerves painfully, producing in my mind alternate sensations of pathetic dejection, so that I was ready to shed tears; and of daring resolution, so that I was inclined to rush into the thickest part of the battle. 'Sir (said he), I should never hear it, if it made me such a fool.'"[76]

It should not surprise us that great revival movements, evangelistic campaigns, and political and nationalistic crusades have all swept forward on the wings of song. Even Israel felt a new sense of unity and victory when they sang God's praises at the Red Sea (Exod. 15), a scene that will be repeated in new dimensions when God's people arrive in heaven (Rev. 15:1-4).

I am convinced that congregations learn more theology (good and bad) from the songs they sing than from the sermons they hear. Many sermons are doctrinally sound and contain a fair amount of biblical information, but they lack that necessary emotional content that gets ahold of the listener's heart. Music, however, reaches the mind and the heart at the same time. It has power to touch and move the emotions, and for that reason can become a wonderful tool in the hands of the Spirit or a terrible weapon in the hands of the Adversary. Naive congregations can sing their way into heresy before they can realize what is going on.

Another reason why music can create problems in the local assembly is the absence of training on the part of the congregation. Most church members consider themselves experts in the area of music, and they do not hesitate to tell the pastor or the minister of music exactly which music is right and which is wrong. Of course, "what is right" is music they personally enjoy; "what is wrong" is music they do not enjoy. It is as simple as that.

But what they are doing is building the   ch music ministry on personal taste and prejudice and not on bib   rinciples. This is not to criticize personal taste, because all of us have personal likes and dislikes when it comes to music. *But there is no explanation for taste.* "Taste by itself, no matter how refined it is, is useless," writes Harold M. Best. "If God senses faith at work, faith which makes us free of conditioned reflexes, he smiles, whatever the supposed level of achievement *at the time.*"[77] The little girl who struggles through her piano solo at the annual Sunday-school program pleases God just as much as the gifted organist playing a difficult fugue during the offertory.

Personally, I do not get a great deal of enjoyment or edification at Sunday-school programs; but I must not permit my personal tastes and prejudices to determine what God can or cannot bless, or even what others can or cannot enjoy. I enjoy classical music, especially the great Christian classics, while other members of my family enjoy "easy listening" music and even "country-western." My wife and I enjoy authentic Chinese food, but we have relatives who will not even attempt to like it. There is no accounting for personal tastes, and we must not make taste the basis for our ministry of music.

Francis Schaeffer says just about the same thing when he discusses *style*. "Let me say firmly that *there is no such thing as a godly style or an ungodly style*. The more one tries to make such a distinction, the more confusing it becomes."[78] But each of us has his or her preferences, and it is easy to make these preferences the law of the Medes and the Persians that cannot be altered. And when you start applying personal tests and tastes to all the elements that make up music—tone, rhythm, melody, lyrics, and so on—you create a hopelessly complicated problem.

EVALUATING MUSIC FOR WORSHIP

All of this suggests that we need some sensible standards to help us evaluate Christian music. Let me suggest five.

1. *Biblical content*. If there is no message in the song, or if the message does not square with orthodox biblical doctrine, then there is no place for it in Christian worship. In my Bible-conference ministry in many places, I have had to endure some most unbiblical music. I have heard well-known artists, some of them quite gifted, sing songs in church that belonged at a Boy Scout campfire or a meeting of a service club. The name of Jesus was not used, and God was referred to only obliquely. When Jesus was mentioned in a song, what was said about Him was vague and sentimental, not theological; and you could have substituted the name "Buddha" or "Zoroaster" without affecting the message of the song.

I am not suggesting that our Christian lyrics use technical theological language (what rhymes with "predestination?"), because we must leave room for creative expression in our religious poetry. But the language we use should express the doctrine we hold, and if it does not, it is not a Christian song. How can the Spirit of God use a song that ignores or contradicts what He wrote in the Bible? After all, when you compare Ephesians 5:18-33 with Colossians 3:16-19, you see that to be filled with the Spirit of God means to be controlled by the Word of God. What are the evidences of being filled with the Spirit? The believer is joyful (Eph. 5:19), thankful (5:20), and submissive (5:21-25). What are the evidences that the believer is filled with the Word of God? He or she is joyful (Col. 3:16), thankful (3:17), and submissive (3:18, 19).

Personally, I have a difficult time believing that a singer is filled with the Spirit if his or her song is not filled with the Word. Some people who think they are filled with the Spirit may only be fooled by the spirits, and this is dangerous. God blesses His Word not our talents.

If a song is biblically sound, it will have a Christian outlook on life, a Christian world view. It will not simply be a worldly song punctuated with biblical phrases, but a biblical song presented in a way that communicates truth to believers and/or a lost world. I have had my fill of religious celebrities and their "pep songs" that exhort me to face the wind, climb the mountain, and keep a smile on my face. My needs are much deeper.

The biblical message in the song must be understandable and presented in a way that may be understood. This also applies to congregational singing. "Sing praises with understanding" (Ps. 47:7). "I will pray with the spirit, and I will also pray with the understanding. I will sing with the spirit, and I will also sing with the understanding" (1 Cor. 14:15). What Paul wrote about his preaching applies to our singing: "in the church I would rather speak five words with my understanding, that I may teach others also, than ten thousand words in a tongue" (1 Cor. 14:19).

It is unfortunate that we have biblically illiterate people in our congregations who may not recognize or understand the scriptural references and allusions in even our great hymns of the church. The pastor and minister of music need to educate their people and relate the hymnal to the Word of God. In one of my pastorates, I did a series of sermons based on the Scriptures that form the foundations for some of the great hymns, and some of the members were amazed that hymns were even based on the Bible![79]

2. *Technical excellence.* No amount of beautiful melody can compensate for poor poetry. At the same time, why should beautiful poetry be wedded to an ugly tune? In the lyrics, the melody, the arrangement, and the presentation (instrumental and vocal), technical excellence is vitally important. Each musician must do his or her very best, and must keep striving to do better. "Play skillfully" is the admonition of Psalm 33:3. No amount of spirituality can compensate for lack of ability, just as no amount of ability can compensate for lack of devotion to Christ.

God wants us to do the best we can with what we have. Most local churches cannot afford to call gifted and trained musicians to direct a ministry of music, and some churches that can afford it have overdone it. I have attended some services where the pastor, as he stood to preach, could well have said, "We interrupt this concert to bring you a sermon." The God Who rejoices at the songs of infants, and even the cries of the birds, will accept the dedicated ministry of even a below-average musician whose heart is right with God.

3. *Spiritual motive.* Only God sees the thoughts and intents of the heart, and we must be careful not to pass judgment. The line between performance and ministry is a fine one, and we must be careful not to cross over and start using our abilities simply to promote ourselves. We believers must pray more for Christians to whom God has given great musical talents, because they face insidious temptations that the rest of us may not encounter in quite the same way. At any rate, all believers, whether in the choir or in the congregation, whether leading or following, need to minister to the glory of God.

4. *Authenticity.* I mean by this that ministry is a true and sincere expression of the person and his culture. I have always appreciated, when visiting the mission fields, sharing in *authentic* expressions of worship rather than imported ones. The Great Commission does not tell us to export our culture or our cultic forms of worship. The living Word of God will of itself, if permitted, generate forms of worship that belong to the people and their culture. This does not mean that one culture cannot borrow from another and thereby enrich its

own religious experience, because we all learn from one another. It simply means that expressions of worship must be authentic, revealing the cultural distinctives of the people.

Once again, it is the Incarnation that encourages this approach to worship. When our Lord came to earth, He entered a definite culture and expressed Himself in terms appreciated and understood by the people of that culture. He related the new to the old and the timeless to the needs of the hour. The early heralds of the gospel followed His example and presented the Word in ways that identified with the cultures of the people who heard that Word.

This does not mean that we "baptize" everything in our culture and claim it for Christ, because there are some practices and values that certainly are not worthy of the gospel. When it comes to planning the church's worship, the leaders must keep their balance lest they permit culture to destroy the Christian testimony or the Christian faith to destroy the culture. Our task is not to transplant our culture in the name of Christ, but to transform their culture by the power of Christ.

But this principle is true of individual Christians within the same culture. Not everyone expresses his faith in the same way, and we must leave room for variety *so long as it expresses authenticity*. My wife and I once worshiped in a Baptist church in the Smoky Mountains, and the service was different from anything we had ever experienced; but it was authentic. The congregation, singers, and pastor were praising God in a manner that suited them perfectly. Had they acted like a Presbyterian congregation on Fifth Avenue, New York, we would have suspected something.

This is not to suggest that there was no room for improvement, or that "This is the way we do it" is the all-embracing excuse that permits anything to happen. The Holy Spirit can use the Word to instruct us, if we are willing, and to show us the better way. But the Spirit will not destroy individuality in order to impose conformity. "The history of Christian worship," writes Frank C. Senn, "is the story of the give and take between cult and culture."[80]

This helps us to understand why ethnic groups prefer to worship together: they share a common culture. My wife and I have a predominantly Scandinavian background and enjoy the worship traditions that belong to that heritage. But we have also learned to appreciate the traditions of other groups, and this has enriched our own worship experience.

5. *Balance*. Even in worship, it is possible to have too much of a good thing. Variety and balance are important if we are to have a healthy worship experience. This is why it is good to follow the Christian Year and pay attention to the great festivals that proclaim our faith history. Without sacrificing his own freedom or ignoring the burden of his own heart, the Spirit-led pastor can guide his flock through the special seasons of the year and still deliver to them God's message for that hour. If I were pastoring a church again, I think I would pay more attention to variety and balance both in the music and the preaching. There were areas of Christian truth and duty that I fear I overlooked because of ignorance or prejudice. I think I would also provide more variety and balance in the Scripture lessons, perhaps even following some adaptation of a pericope.

Finally, I think I would also pay more attention to the *setting* of worship. I realize the dangers that are involved when we get too concerned about "atmosphere," but perhaps we could afford to take a few risks! "All the arts can make a contribution to Christian worship," writes Frank C. Senn. "But this is not the same as saying that liturgy is an art form."[81] The arts can help us to express our worship, but we must take care not to worship the arts. This is "religious aestheticism" and it breeds a cult that caters to taste instead of to truth.

Man himself is a work of art, made in the image of God. The world in which man lives is a work of art, declaring the glory and wisdom of God. The church is God's "poem" (Eph. 2:10—*poiēma*, "workmanship") and is being created after His masterplan. Our worship ought to make the best use of all the wonderful materials He has given us—truth, people, material objects, sounds, smells, foods, and skillful arts. All things can and should be sanctified by the Word of God and prayer and made suitable for the Master's use. "Let them praise the name of the LORD, for He commanded and they were created" (Ps. 148:5).

GRACIOUS FATHER,

Forgive me for being so blind and deaf. Your universe is one vast cathedral of praise, and yet I have not seen it or heard it as I should have, and I have been the poorer because of my ignorance.

All things You have created praise Your name. And all of creation can be used by Your church to worship You. Thank You, Father, for this treasury of blessing.

Thank You, too, for the gifted people You have given to Your church to help us use the arts to worship and serve You. May it be the Creator, not the creature, that receives the glory.

May we truly worship You in beauty. Your world is filled with beauty. You are infinitely original and the variety of Your creation amazes me. Deliver us from sameness as we praise Your Name. Be pleased to guide us into true creativity, and save us from novelty.

In Jesus' Name,
AMEN.

PART IV

Worship Involves Warfare

Let the high praises of God be in their
mouth, and a two-edged sword in their
hand.
PSALM 149:6

In this Israel was not an example, but a
type; we will not copy the chosen people in
making literal war, but we will fulfill the
emblem by carrying on spiritual war.
CHARLES HADDON SPURGEON[82]

Who is this King of glory?
The LORD strong and mighty,
The LORD mighty in battle.
PSALM 24:8

But You have cast us off and put us to
shame, and You do not go out with our
armies.
PSALM 44:9

CHAPTER 13 *In which we recover a neglected fact about Satan and learn about spiritual warfare*

GOD AND SATAN have this in common: each desires our worship. God wants us to worship Him because He is worthy and He graciously wants to transform us. Satan wants our worship because he wants to destroy us, and worship is the easiest way to achieve that diabolical purpose. This explains why worship involves warfare: whenever we bow to worship God, the Adversary will oppose us.

GOD'S RIVAL

The Bible does not shed much light on the origin of Satan. Many scholars believe that Isaiah 14:12–15 goes beyond the immediate reference to the king of Babylon and applies to Satan. If so, then a desire for worship (which is basically pride) was the sin that brought about Lucifer's fall. "I will ascend above the heights of the clouds, I will be like the Most High" (Isa. 14:14). Apparently a number of angelic creatures were willing to worship Lucifer, and they fell with him. This satanic army opposes God and His people and can only be defeated by God-given spiritual means.

When Satan tempted our first parents, his appeal was centered on worship. His approach was to question God's Word ("Has God indeed said . . . ," Gen. 3:1), deny God's Word ("You will not surely die," v. 4), and then substitute His own promise ("You will be like God," v. 5).

There is no missing the parallel between Lucifer's "I will be like the Most High!" and the deceptive promise "You will be like God." When Adam and Eve partook of the fruit, they "exchanged the truth of God for the lie, and worshiped and served the creature rather than the Creator" (Rom. 1:25). Satan received the worship that he was seeking, and he is still receiving it wherever people substitute the creature for the Creator and believe the lie that they can be their own god.

We noted at the beginning of this pilgrimage that humility is important to true spiritual worship. Pride is the essential ingredient when it comes to worshiping Satan. Lucifer's repeated "I will!" in Isaiah 14 is evidence enough of his pride and is in contrast to our Lord's repeated statement in the garden, "Nevertheless, not what I will, but what You will" (Mark 14:36). And the fall of Lucifer must be contrasted with our Lord's deliberate self-humbling described in Philippians 2:1-11. Lucifer exalted himself and was humiliated; Christ humbled Himself and was highly exalted.

"So far as . . . worship [of Christ] is genuine and complete, pride is eliminated," wrote William Temple; "for He whom we worship is humility itself incarnate."[83]

It is this truth that helps us better understand Cain and Abel and their worship of God. Both brothers believed in God and both came to the altar to worship, but only Abel's worship was accepted by God. Satan is a liar and a murderer (John 8:44) and so was Cain: he murdered his own brother and then lied about it to God (Gen. 4:1-15). First John 3:12 informs us that Cain "was of the wicked one and murdered his brother. And why did he murder him? Because his works were evil and his brother's righteous." "The sacrifice of the wicked is an abomination to the LORD, but the prayer of the upright is His delight" (Prov. 15:8).

The character of our worship depends on the condition of our heart, for "without faith it is impossible to please Him" (Heb. 11:6). It was Abel's faith that made his worship acceptable to God (v. 4). In humility, he accepted what God had said, believed it, and acted upon it. He brought to the altar a humble sacrifice of faith and God bore witness that he had been accepted.

Throughout the Old Testament, there is a clear record of the lines of Cain and Abel, unbelief and faith, Satan and God. Satan's religion is the religion of substitutes: worship anyone or anything but the true God. He enticed Israel to worship the idols of the pagan nations that they conquered. Paul makes it clear that idol worship is actually demonic and is really Satan worship (1 Cor. 10:14-22). So much for comparative religions.

When Satan tempted our Lord in the wilderness, he offered Him all the kingdoms of the world in return for one act of worship. "All these things I will give You if You will fall down and worship me" (Matt. 4:9), and the verb tense indicates a single act of worship. Satan did not ask for *service;* but he certainly knew that whatever a person worships, he serves. That explains our Lord's reply, "You shall worship the LORD your God, and Him only you shall serve" (v. 10; see also Deut. 6:13; 10:20).

One day Satan will make that same offer to another, and it will be accepted; and that person will become the world leader that the Scriptures call "the man of sin . . . the son of perdition, who opposes and exalts himself above all that is called God or that is worshiped, so that he sits as God in the temple of God, showing himself that he is God" (2 Thess. 2:3, 4). According to Revelation 13, this "man of sin" will bring about the worship of Satan by the whole world, except, of course, those who belong to Christ and are sealed by Him.

The fact that Satan has always wanted worship helps us to understand his hatred for Israel, God's chosen people who have given witness to the true God. It also explains Satan's hatred for the church, the believing saints "who worship God in the Spirit, rejoice in Christ Jesus, and have no confidence in the flesh" (Phil. 3:3). Our spiritual worship of God hinders Satan's work, defeats his plans, robs him of territory, and increases his hatred of God and God's people. So long as the church does not worship God in the Spirit, Satan is happy to let us do anything else we want to do; for he knows that all of our man-made programs, no matter how seemingly successful, can never storm the gates of hell and defeat his demonic armies.[84]

GOD'S WORSHIPING WARRIORS

A worshiping church must of necessity be a warring church, for true worship is spiritual warfare. The best example of this truth is seen in the nation of Israel. From the hour that Israel was delivered by God from the bondage of Egypt, the nation was constituted a holy army for the Lord. "And it came to pass, on that very same day, that the LORD brought the children of Israel out of the land of Egypt according to their armies" (Exod. 12:51). The nation's song of triumph at the Red Sea announced without apology, "The LORD is a man of war; the LORD is His name" (15:3). Whenever the camp of Israel moved, the procession was like that of a well-organized army, with the ark of God leading the way and Moses saying: "Rise up, O LORD! Let Your enemies be scattered, and let those who hate You flee before You" (Num. 10:35).

In short, Israel was a worshiping army, fighting the battles of the Lord. The success of their warfare depended on the success of their worship. If they were "right with God," they had no difficulty defeating their enemies. If they were not pleasing to God, they were shamefully defeated. It was as simple as that. It was then that Israel lamented, "You do not go out with our armies!" (Ps. 44:9).

When the nation took a census, it was based on availability for battle, "all who are able to go to war in Israel" (Num. 1:3). To lose a battle meant much more than national disgrace; it robbed Jehovah of the glory due to His name. After all, He is "the LORD of hosts," the Lord of the armies.

The center of the camp was dedicated to the Lord, for that is where the tabernacle stood. Faithful ministry in the tabernacle was essential for victory on the battlefield. Israel's shameful defeat before the Philistines was caused partly by the unfaithfulness of the priests (1 Sam. 4). Even though they carried the ark of God out to the battlefield, God did not honor them with victory. What they did was not an act of faith; it was only superstition.

It is interesting to note that a group of women "assembled at the door of the tabernacle of meeting" (Exod. 38:8). The Hebrew word translated "assembled" has a definite military flavor to it. Literally it means "assembled by troops at the door of the tabernacle of meeting." In 2 Kings 25:19 and Jeremiah 52:25, the word refers to the mustering of troops.

But even more interesting is the fact that this same word is used of the ministry of the priests and Levites in the tabernacle. "To perform the service" in Numbers 4:23 and 8:24 literally means "to war the warfare." The spiritual battle was fought at the tabernacle; the physical battle was waged in the field.

Soon after Israel's exodus from Egypt, the people learned firsthand the importance of winning the spiritual victory. The Amalekites attacked Israel, but God gave the nation victory because Moses, holding the rod of God, stood on the mountain and interceded with God

(Exod. 17:8–16). It took both Joshua with his sword and Moses with his uplifted rod to defeat the enemy.

The militant spirit permeates the book of Psalms. Psalm 1 magnifies the God of blessing, while Psalm 2 extols the God of battles; and the two go together. It is because Israel obeys the law that God gives her victory over her enemies. Psalm 68 is one of the most militant of the psalms, describing God's conquest of His enemies. "Let God arise, let His enemies be scattered; let those also who hate Him flee before Him" (v. 1). "You have ascended on high, You have led captivity captive" (v. 18). We shall see in our next chapter how the New Testament church borrowed these psalms and applied them to the victories of Christ.

David's praise in Psalm 144 certainly would perplex a pacifist! He actually blesses God for training his hands for war! In v. 9, he lays aside his sword and picks up his harp; the soldier becomes the singer. Again, it is the blending of worship and warfare. "Let the high praises of God be in their mouth, and a two-edged sword in their hand" (Ps. 149:6).

Perhaps the most dramatic illustration of worship and warfare is seen in Jehosaphat's confrontation with the Moabites and the Ammonites, as recorded in 2 Chronicles 20. The first step the king took was to call a fast and gather the people together for prayer. In that prayer, Jehoshaphat reminded the Lord of His promises and His past performances on behalf of the people of Israel. The result was a Spirit-given message from the priest Jahaziel that God would give them the victory.

The next day, the king assembled the people for battle, but he did a strange thing: he put the singers ahead of the soldiers! (Perhaps there are some pastors who would like to send some choir members into the front lines.) "And when he had consulted with the people, he appointed those who should sing to the LORD, and who should praise the beauty of holiness, as they went out before the army and were saying; 'Praise the LORD, for His mercy endures forever'" (v. 21).

The result? God caused the invading armies to defeat each other! Jehoshaphat and his people did not need to fight at all! They simply claimed the spoils and returned to Jerusalem for a great praise service at the temple.

During Jeremiah's day, the people were sure God would protect them from Babylon because the temple of the Lord was in Jerusalem, and He would never permit His house to be destroyed. The temple services were going on as usual and the false prophets were announcing peace and security. But Jeremiah knew that the worship at the temple was hypocritical and superstitious. "Do not trust in these lying words, saying, 'The temple of the LORD, the temple of the LORD, the temple of the LORD are these'" (Jer. 7:4). "Behold, you trust in lying words that cannot profit" (v. 8). Then he gave them God's perspective on the matter. "Has this house, which is called by My name, become a den of thieves in your eyes?" (v. 11).

The frightening thing is that, to all appearances, this was a time of great religious revival. The temple had been repaired and the God-given ceremonies restored, and the people were rejoicing in these blessings. Jeremiah's message of repentance and judgment sounded out of place against the joyful sounds of the temple choirs and the encouraging messages of the prophets.

Yes, "national religion" was at an all-time high in popularity but it was not sincerely coming from the hearts of the people. They broke God's law and then went to the temple to share in God's blessing! They made the temple a "a den of thieves"—the place that thieves run to when they want to hide! The prophets, priests, and people were using public religion as a cover-up for their private sins!

The nation fell to the Babylonians. The temple was desecrated and then destroyed. Why? Because true worship had disappeared from the land. Religion was popular, but it was not penetrating. It was a veneer that covered the rotting foundations of the nation. The people fooled each other, but they could not fool God or His true servant, Jeremiah.

The sad thing is that the prophets were to blame. In his Lamentations, Jeremiah wrote: "Your prophets have seen for you false and deceptive visions; they have not uncovered your iniquity, to bring back your captives, but have envisioned for you false prophecies and delusions" (2:14). Disaster had come upon Jerusalem "because of the sins of her prophets and the iniquities of her priests, who shed in her midst the blood of the just" (4:13).

This is a sobering message to us today.

LORD OF HOSTS,

Your son has won for me that decisive victory over Satan and all his hosts. He has "disarmed principalities and powers." Hallelujah!

I realize now, O Lord, that there is a militant side to worship. You are calling me to have Your praises on my lips and Your sword in my hand. The enemy is subtle and strong, and I cannot win the battle in my own strength.

Help me to remember that my battle is not against flesh and blood, but against the rulers of darkness and the hosts of spiritual wickedness. May I not depend on the arm of flesh. The weapons of this warfare are not fleshly, but spiritual.

O Lord, help Your church to be a conquering army! May we not trust the externals—our budgets, our buildings, our impressive statistics. May we trust You and have clean hands and pure hearts so that You might fight our battles with us. And remind us that we are not fighting flesh and blood; we are fighting spiritual wickedness.

O Lord, give us unity. May we fight the enemy and not each other. Help us to be more than conquerors through Jesus Christ our Lord!

AMEN.

CHAPTER 14 *In which we discover that God's church today is a spiritual army*

I UNDERSTAND THAT evangelist D. L. Moody did not like his soloist Ira Sankey to use the popular song "Onward Christian Soldiers" in their campaigns, because Moody felt the church was a poor excuse for an army. He was probably right. If being a good soldier involves obedience, discipline, and sacrifice, then many Christians have either never enlisted or have gone AWOL.

And yet our Lord's first mention of the church made it clear that believers are involved in a battle: "On this rock I will build my church, and the gates of Hades shall not prevail against it" (Matt. 16:18). In Isaiah 38:10, the phrase "gates of Sheol" [the Hebrew equivalent of "Hades"] refers to death; so our Lord's words can mean, "The church will never be swallowed up by death." However, in the Old Testament, "gates" usually refer to places of power and authority. The elders of the city met at the gates to transact their business. So, the phrase "gates of Hades" probably means "the very power and authority of Satan."

It did not take Peter long to discover that Satan was very much at work! Peter privately advised Jesus not to go to the cross, and the Savior replied, "Get behind me, Satan!"

The history of the church is the story of believing people storming the gates of hell and delivering those held in sin's bondage. The military images used of the church in the New Testament ought to convince us that the Christian life is more than joyful fellowship or quiet meditation. It is a battle that we cannot escape and that we dare not lose; and the key to our victory is worship.

In his "Epistle to the Ephesians," Ignatius of Antioch (died c. 110) wrote:

Take heed, then, often to come together to give thanks to God, and show forth His praise. For when ye come frequently together in the same place, the powers of Satan are destroyed, and his "fiery darts" urging to sin fall back ineffectual. For your concord and harmonious faith prove his destruction, and the torment of his assistants.[85]

I wonder how many believers today see corporate worship as a major weapon in defeating the armies of hell?

ARMED FOR THE BATTLE

Living as he did in a military state, and knowing as he did the spiritual battle in which he was engaged, the apostle Paul often used military imagery when he communicated with both churches and pastors. In fact, along with athletics, architecture, and anatomy, the army is one of Paul's favorite figures.

Ephesians 6:10-20 is a key text, pointing out that Satan and his demonic hosts are the enemy, but God has given us the equipment necessary for successful attack and defense. The image of "spiritual armor" is also used in Romans 13:11-13, 2 Corinthians 6:7 and 10:2-6, and 1 Thessalonians 5:5-8. God expects us to wear this armor, yet many believers ignore it completely.

Each morning, as I begin my devotional time, I "put on" the individual pieces of the armor by faith. I ask the Lord to equip me so that the *whole* armor covers me. I want my mind protected by the helmet of salvation and my heart covered by the breastplate of righteousness. I want my actions controlled by the girdle of truth, and I want to walk wearing the shoes of peace, so that I will be a peacemaker and not a troublemaker. By faith I take the Word of God, the Spirit's sword, and I wield it against the attacks of the wicked one. Then I pray for God's power to enable me, for equipment without enablement means defeat.

All of this is a spiritual exercise that I do each day by faith. No special feelings are involved. I simply take God at His Word and, through prayer, dress myself in the spiritual armor He has provided. Theologically, I suppose this image simply means identifying myself with all that Christ is and all that He has accomplished for me. I appropriate for myself what God has told me is freely available to me. I can testify that doing this as a part of my devotional disciplines has made a difference in my life and ministry.

All believers are soldiers in God's army, whether they know it or not and whether they act like it or not. We share in the triumph of our Lord (2 Cor. 2:14–16 and Col. 2:15). As His soldiers, we must be devoted to Him and obedient in duty (2 Tim. 2:3–4). Even the resurrection is pictured in military terms, for the word *order* in 1 Corinthians 15:23 means "a military company."

One of Paul's favorite words is *parangellō*, which refers to a military order handed down from the commander. Paul ordered Timothy to stay on duty in Ephesus and fight a good battle (1 Tim. 1:18), keeping God's commandments (6:13). Timothy in turn was to command the church as he taught the Word (1:3; 4:11; 5:7; 6:17); moreover, he was to *guard* what he had learned from Paul so that the truth could be passed on to others (6:20; 2 Tim. 1:14).

The church must keep in mind, however, that we are fighting a spiritual battle, using spiritual weapons. "For the weapons of our warfare are not carnal but mighty in God for pulling down strongholds, casting down arguments and every high thing that exalts itself against the knowledge of God, bringing every thought into captivity to the obedience of Christ" (2 Cor. 10:4, 5). The battle is within the minds, hearts, and wills of men; and only the Word of God and prayer can prevail. The early church was a worshiping church; therefore it was a winning church. "But we will give ourselves continually to prayer and to the ministry of the word" (Acts. 6:4).

Unless you and I are worshiping Christians, and unless our congregations are worshiping assemblies, there is no hope for victory over Satan, no matter what the statistics may show. "I hope I am wrong," writes Michael Green, "but I do not see the modern church, in the West at any rate, as a body which is alive to spiritual warfare. It seems pretty preoccupied with its own survival, its petty concerns, its tradition, its canons and its revised worship books—or else coming out with dicta about many of the contemporary problems of our society without getting to the heart of the matter."[86]

The heart of the matter, of course, is the spiritual conflict that we must engage in because we worship the true and living God. Satan does not care what the church does so long as it does not worship. Once the church really begins to worship, then Satan's territory is under attack and he is in danger of losing some of his spoils. This is an obvious truth, and yet few Christians seem to know it. It seems incredible, but in all of the books I have read about worship, I have found little or nothing about Satan; and in all of the books I have read about Satan, I have found little or nothing about worship! No wonder he is winning the war!

WORSHIP AND WARFARE

If we have failed to notice the worship/warfare theme in the rest of the Bible, we surely cannot miss it when we read the last book in the Bible, the book of Revelation. In fact, the book of Revelation deals with the three aspects of worship that we have been examining in this pilgrimage: *wonder, witness, and warfare.* The whole book is filled with the wonders John beheld as he was in the Spirit on the Lord's Day. The word *witness* is a key word in Revelation, used at least eighteen times in the Greek text as either a noun or verb. *War* is referred to at least eight times, and *worship* is used twenty-four times. It is a book about spiritual worship that reveals itself in wonder, witness and warfare. It is also the book of the *throne;* the word is used forty-six times! God exercises His sovereignty when His people worship. At least nine times in this book, God is called *Pantokratōr*—"the Almighty!"

Perhaps one reason why God is not exercising His almighty power on our behalf today is because we have neglected worship. It would do our churches good to meditate on the worship scenes in the book of Revelation, and to notice that as the church worshiped, God gave His people power for witness and warfare.

No matter what view you may take of prophecy, you must admit that Revelation contrasts true and false worship. Satan commands people to worship him, while God commands people to worship Him. Most of the world follows Satan because he guarantees to take care of all those who worship him. They will have food to eat, for one thing, and they will belong to the "popular majority." "Skin for skin! Yes, all that a man has he will give for his life" has always been Satan's philosophy (Job 2:4). It will prove true for most of the world's population when God permits Satan to take over.

Satan's attack against Job really was in the sphere of worship. Satan's argument was that Job worshiped God only because God blessed and protected His servant. If God took away all His blessings, Job would stop blessing God and would begin to curse Him. The great question in the book of Job is not "Why do the righteous suffer?" but "Is our God worth worshiping even if He does not bless us the way we think He should?" The three Hebrews of Daniel 3 faced the same decision, and they stood firmly for the truth. *They did not know for sure that God would deliver them!* "Our God . . . is able to deliver us," they affirmed. ". . . but if [He does] not, let it be known to you, O king, that we do not serve your gods, nor will we worship the gold image which you have set up" (Dan. 3:17, 18). They were not for sale.

Why do we worship God today? Because He is worthy! Because worship is the only way we can witness for Him and fight His battles. As we worship Him, He transforms us—and our churches—and we become worshiping, witnessing warriors who fight the battles of the Lord for His glory! Christ has made us His "kings and priests" (Rev. 1:6) and we dare not separate the throne from the altar. *We reign as we worship.* We exercise His authority as we honor His majesty.

THE THREAT OF UNWITTING DEFEAT

This is not the place to deal with the messages to the seven churches. I only want to point out that the last of the churches, Laodicea, seems to fit our church situation at present. The average congregation today may appear to be lukewarm about spiritual things; and yet that same congregation will boast of its financial and material sufficiency. (Again, why is it that church letterheads and bulletin covers usually picture *buildings?*) The early church had neither money nor buildings (nor letterheads, for that matter), and yet it conquered the greatest military and political machine of history, the Roman Empire.

Jesus said to the Laodicean church members, "You are wretched, miserable, poor, blind, and naked" (Rev. 3:17). *This is a picture of a defeated army!* A conquering army would often humiliate a defeated foe by stripping the soldiers and forcing them to walk partly or completely naked while the victors claimed the spoils. Sometimes the captives would have their eyes gouged out. Our Lord saw the Laodicean church as a defeated army *that did not know it was defeated.* That may be the situation our churches are in today.

What is the solution to the problem? John gives us the answer; for after he told the seven churches what they were like, he revealed to them the throne room of heaven where the heavenly hosts were worshiping the Lord. We have already examined Revelation 4 and 5, so there is no need to repeat its lessons. What I do need to repeat and emphasize is the plain fact that, in the book of Revelation, the bridge between the messages to the churches (chapters 2 and 3) and the conflict between Christ and Satan (chapters 6 through 19) is the worship of God by His people. We are unprepared for the battlefield if we have not lingered to worship in the throne room.

I have nearly four shelves of books in my library devoted to prophecy and the book of Revelation, and I have even written a brief commentary on Revelation myself. But I wonder if we have not been so caught up in the *predictive* aspect of this marvelous book that we have forgotten or neglected the *prescriptive* aspect. Things are not going to get easier for God's people, and we are not ready for the battle. We are so concerned with comfort, security, and peace of mind that we are totally unprepared for "the fiery trial" that is sure to come.

We are not warriors because we are not worshipers.

I trust it is not too late to change.

LOVING FATHER,

I hardly know how to pray. Here I thought I was doing so well in my Christian life, and now I see myself as a defeated soldier. I thought I was "in need of nothing" when, in reality, I am in need of everything!

You have made me, in Christ, a king and a priest. The throne and the altar must stay together, for I can "reign in life" only as I worship.

Keep me from a commercial faith that barters for blessings. Keep me from a comfortable faith that refuses to confront the enemy. May I, by Your grace, maintain that delicate balance "within the veil" and "without the camp."

Through Jesus Christ,
AMEN.

CHAPTER 15 *In which we must make a difficult decision*

WORSHIP IS NOT an option, it is an obligation; it is not a luxury, it is a necessity. The one thing that the church can do *that no other assembly can do* is to worship God and glorify Him. I am not sure that we are doing it.

William Temple said, "This world can be saved from political chaos and collapse by one thing only, and that is worship."[87] The only hope for the world is the church, and the only hope for the church is a return to worship. God must transform His people and His church before he can work through us to meet the crushing needs of a world lost in sin. As I said at the beginning of our pilgrimage, every ministry of the church should be a by-product of worship. Ministry that is divorced from worship has no roots and therefore can produce no lasting fruits.

It is not a matter of either/or. No church abandons evangelism, for example, when it returns to worship. Rather, it enriches that evangelism and gives it spiritual depth. A return to worship does not destroy good Christian fellowship. If anything, it puts that fellowship on a more solid foundation than coffee and donuts or tea and cookies.

However, I would not lead you to believe that a return to worship is any easy thing. It is not.

For one thing, human nature being what it is, we do not *naturally* want to seek after God and get nearer to Him. Only the Holy Spirit of God can create within us the deep desire to worship, to give to God our total loving adoration. Before the Spirit can bring us to that place, we must deal with our sins; and dealing with sin is not an easy task.

Another obstacle is our seeming success. "The church is going along fine," say the officers, "and the bills are being paid. Why upset things?" Whenever I discuss worship with people, I often hear, "But some of the greatest churches in America know little about worship, and God is blessing them." Only God knows what is really going on in *any* church. The concerns I have shared in this book are based on my own limited observations, and I cannot guarantee that they are the viewpoint of heaven. But I have a feeling that all is not well even with some of the "success" churches.

More and more, some of the "great churches" are having a difficult time finding "great pastors" to fill their pulpits. In many cities, believers drift from church to church, looking for "deep teaching" rather than practical Christian living. Which church they wind up in depends on who is in the pulpit, and today there is a galaxy of evangelical celebrities that are sure to draw a crowd. The fact that some of them may not have the best track record in their homes or personal lives does not seem important to the church member seeking an evening's entertainment.

A return to worship could be a threat to the preacher who enjoys being important and playing God in the lives of his people. Or to the preacher who has perfected a sermon system that gives him an acceptable outline week after week. Or to the preacher who is a good platform man and can keep things moving so that the congregation is interested and entertained.

A return to worship can be a threat to the church musician who would rather perform than minister, and who has no intention of bringing his weekday life into line with his Sunday profession.

A return to worship could be a threat to the church member who does not want to be disturbed. He fills a place faithfully week after week, he pays his tithes, and he does a job in the church now and then; but what happens at the church has no relationship with the rest of his life. He is getting by—and that is all that counts.

WHAT WILL IT TAKE

What will it take to motivate us to worship God? What will have to happen before we will dismantle our shabby religious sideshows and build once again an altar to the Lord?

The greatest judgment God could pass on the churches today would be to take His hands off and let them go right on doing what they are doing. I once heard A. W. Tozer say, "If God took His Holy

Spirit out of this world, what we are doing would go right on *and nobody would know the difference.*"

I pray that God in His mercy will not abandon us but will give us another opportunity. We have been living on substitutes for so long that if a revival of worship ever did come, many of God's people would probably see it as a threat to the gospel! Do we really *want* to worship God? Are we really *willing* to give up our religious toys and get down to business with Him? Can we sincerely abandon our pragmatic views of church ministry ("Well, it works! You can't argue with success!") and get back to the biblical vision of God?

Perhaps God will not leave us where we are. Perhaps He will permit an economic crisis that will force churches to examine their priorities and get back to the things that matter most. Perhaps He will permit persecution, a "fiery trial" that will separate the gold from the dross. The day may come when it will not be too popular to belong to an evangelical church and when evangelicalism will not have the patronage of people in high places.

Or perhaps God will deal with individual believers here and there, honest people who confess their desperate need for spiritual reality. Perhaps He will whisper to some of these hungry souls who are not satisfied with religious routine week after week, who sincerely want to worship God and experience His transforming power. He may draw near to these few hardy saints who fear God more than they fear social pressure and who are not threatened by change.

In fact, you could be one of those saints.

God changes churches by changing individuals. John Wesley's heart was strangely warmed, and the result was a revival that delivered England from the bloodbath that almost destroyed France. Church history is filled with the names of men and women who transformed churches and ministered to the world because they permitted God to transform them. They were worshipers and warriors, and God used them.

They were transformers, not conformers. Their lives were controlled by power from within, not pressure from without.

They were misunderstood and criticized; they were even arrested and killed. Their biggest enemy was the religious establishment of their day, the successful religious leaders who had long ago lost touch with spiritual reality and were only living on their reputations.

But, where do you begin?

You begin in your own home, in your own personal devotional life. You start each day with God—not reading a quick verse-prayer-and-poem devotional, but spending time in His Word, in meditation and worship, and in prayer.

Time. That is where the rub comes in. We do not "take time to be holy." We are satisfied with "religious fast food" that is packaged for quick and easy consumption. Perhaps "fast food" is better than nothing at all, but is a poor substitute for the real thing.

True worship takes time, and one of the evidences that we are starting to make spiritual progress in our worship is the calmness that comes to the soul as you wait before God. You are conscious of time but not controlled by time. You enjoy waiting before the Lord and reveling in His wonder and His greatness.

Is this kind of growing experience only for the great saints and mystics? Of course not! It was a fisherman who wrote "And we beheld His glory" (John 1:14). And another fisherman wrote, "Though now you do not see Him, yet believing, you rejoice with joy inexpressible and full of glory" (1 Pet. 1:8). Remember the words of your Savior: "I thank You, Father, Lord of heaven and earth, that You have hidden these things from the wise and prudent and have revealed them to babes" (Matt. 11:25).

We must begin with our own lives, our own personal worship of God. And as we grow, we must not become critical of others and go around trying to change everything at the church. Real spiritual transformation must come from the inside out. We must beware of mere cosmetic changes that do not affect the heart of the church. Singing different hymns, rearranging the order of the service, even rearranging the church furniture, will never produce a transforming church. The Spirit must work in hearts, and that takes time.

Nor should we become what Evelyn Underhill calls "spiritual highbrows" who condescend to worship with the ignorant and unspiritual, but who would rather be elsewhere enjoying the rich atmosphere of a "true" worship service. Our Lord, when on earth, attended the synagogue and the temple, even though both were in the hands of religious leaders who resisted the truth. A spiritual transformer can enter into even a children's Sunday school worship and experience blessing *and be a blessing*. A transformer is always worshiping God, always hungering and thirsting for more of God's grace and glory, and always open to whatever spiritual influences the Father may bring to his or her life.

Yes, we begin with *ourselves*, and we let God work in and through us in His own special way. We avoid copying other saints and, by faith, permit God to develop us in His way. We also avoid copying other churches, knowing that each local assembly must fulfill its own special calling. It took me years to discover that the pronouns in Philippians 2:12, 13 are *plural:* "Work out your own salvation with fear and trembling, for it is God who works in you both to will and to do for His good pleasure." Paul was writing to the entire congregation.

TAKE THE LEAD

Perhaps you are a pastor, and you are yearning for your church to develop a hunger and thirst for spiritual reality. You want them to worship God and become transformers, so that the church can truly minister to the needs that you see all around you and across the world. What do you do?

I think the above counsel applies to you and the leaders who work with you: be sure your own worship experience is living and growing. If it is, there will be a new emphasis and enrichment in your leading of public worship as well as in your pastoral ministry in the home or hospital. Jealously guard your personal time with the Lord each day. Practice spiritual discipline. This means, of course, setting some priorities and learning how to say no; but that is the price to pay. *You cannot be a transformer and always please everybody, nor should you try.*

I have pastored three churches and have had the privilege of ministering to many pastors and Christian workers in conferences in many parts of the world. One of the problems that I see is that ministers are carrying too much luggage. Over the years, they have picked up various tasks, memberships, associations, and so on, and they are trying to carry them all and perform their ministry at the same time.

This extra luggage takes time to organize and energy to carry, and it is costly.

If worship does nothing else for us, it helps us discover the things that are important; and no one needs that more than the pastor or Christian worker. It takes courage, but we simply must get rid of the extra luggage and start carrying only the burdens that He assigns to us. This does not mean eliminating bad things from our lives, because there ought not to be any bad things! It means saying good-bye to good things, enjoyable things, even successful things, because they are getting in our way and robbing us of the time and energy we need to seek after God and serve Him.

Once you have your own life balanced before God, you can start to lead others in your church to worship God and seek His face. It will take time, so be patient. People do not want to change. Teach them tenderly and set the example before them. Some people will leave your fellowship and go where it is safer, but do not be discouraged. Know that you are in the will of God when you are seeking to bring your people closer to Him in their worship experience. Satan will oppose you, but God will vindicate you.

Just be sure that your preaching is an act of worship, and that you prepare each message and each service so as to "proclaim the praises of Him who called you out of darkness into His marvelous light" (1 Pet. 2:9). Keep in mind that the harvest is not the end of the meeting: it is the end of the age. Minister by faith. God promises to do the rest.

Let me close with a penetrating quotation from one of my favorite preachers, Frederick W. Robertson:

Again, it is not a thing which a man can decide, whether he will be a worshiper or not, a worshiper he *must* be, the only question is *what* will he worship? Every man worships—is a born worshiper.[88]

GRACIOUS FATHER,

I have made my decision: I will, by Your grace, worship You and seek to glorify Your name.

Please make me a transformer. May I be used by Your Spirit to make a difference wherever I am.

Deliver me from seeking "an experience." Help me to hunger and thirst after righteousness, to seek Your face, and not to try to duplicate whatever You have done for others.

Give me discernment, lest Satan detour me and I become attracted by whatever substitutes he will offer.

May I be transformed, and may Your church be transformed! And may great glory come to Your Name as saints unite in worship and sinners trust the Savior!

Through Christ our Lord,
AMEN.

APPENDIX 1 *In which we try to answer some questions*

In public and private discussions about worship, often the same questions and comments come up; so it seems wise to deal with some of them here.

1. Our church is very aggressive and evangelistic, and the people are scared to death of liturgy and things like that. How do you explain our success, and what changes would you make?

Every church has a liturgy, whether the congregation likes it or not. A liturgy is simply an order of service. You need one if a group of people is going to try to do something together; otherwise, you would have chaos. I have preached in many churches of the kind you described, and I can assure you that they have a definite liturgy.

The focus of the liturgy, however, does not seem to be the worship of God. It appears to be (and I may be wrong) the conviction of lost sinners so that they will come forward and trust Christ. Please understand that I am not opposed to evangelism or even to public invitations that are led by the Spirit of God. But I do believe that evangelism is a by-product of worship, not a substitute for worship.

As for the "success" of these churches, it all depends on how you measure the ministry. In Revelation 2 and 3, the churches that people thought were failures were praised by the Lord, and the churches that thought they were successful were warned by Him. "Therefore judge nothing before the time, until the Lord comes, who will both bring to light the hidden things of darkness and reveal the counsels of the hearts. Then each one's praise will come from God" (1 Cor. 4:5).

How would I change these churches? If I were called to be pastor, I would simply introduce worship and gently teach the leaders and the people in the pews what I have written in this book. I certainly would not eliminate the evangelistic outreach or burden! I would simply put it into the place where it belongs. After all, leading lost souls to Christ is an act of worship (Rom. 15:15, 16), and true worship does involve witness. I would caution soul-winners to watch their motives so that God's glory, not man's statistics, would be uppermost.

Let me add that there are aggressively evangelistic churches that *do* emphasize and practice worship. Evangelism and worship and not enemies; they are friends.

2. Our pastor and worship committee are always making changes, and this has become confusing to us in the pews. What should we do?

It sounds like your pastor and committee members are trying to *manufacture* effective worship, and this will never work. Someone has called these days "the era of paperback liturgies," and I fear it is true. Something new is always coming out and there are plenty of people ready to grab it and try to use it.

Change for the sake of change is *novelty;* change for the sake of growth is *progress.* Worship committees that deal only with the accidentals, and not the essentials, can never bring about renewal in worship. We are dealing, after all, with theology (what we believe) and not just liturgy (how we will worship).

Pray for your pastor and the committee and co-operate when you can. Perhaps a loving word of counsel and encouragement would be appropriate. Alfred North Whitehead used to say that real progress comes from change in the midst of order and order in the midst of change. Good counsel!

3. Occasionally we have visitors in our church who will hold up their hands during prayer (yes, I confess that I am watching!) or during the singing of a hymn. I find this very distracting. What should we do?

There is nothing wrong with uplifted hands during prayer. In fact, this was the way most Jews prayed. "Lift up your hands in the sanctuary, and bless the LORD" (Ps. 134:2). "Let my prayer be set before You as incense, the lifting up of my hands as the evening sacrifice" (141:2). When Solomon dedicated the temple, he "stood before the altar of the LORD in the presence of all the assembly of Israel, and spread out his hands toward heaven" (1 Kings 8:22). Ezra fell on his knees and spread out his hands when he confessed the sins of the nation (Ezra 9:5).

I might add that our practice of folding our hands in prayer is not necessarily biblical, or even putting our hands together as in the famous "Praying Hands" picture. I am not saying that these practices are wrong, but only that they have no biblical precedent.

As for lifting our hands when we praise God, if it is a natural response from the Spirit, I see nothing wrong with it. When we lift our hands in prayer, it is a symbol of our faith in God, that He will give us what we need. When we lift our hands in praise, it is a symbol that we give everything to God because we love Him. The important thing is that we not call attention to ourselves in such a way that others might be distracted.

A Spirit-filled worshiper is not likely to create problems in a local church, so I suggest you not become critical. The fruit of the Spirit is love. According to 1 Timothy 2:8, nobody should lift up his or her hands if those hands are defiled because of sin, if the person is angry with someone, or is causing trouble in the church. I like the Williams translation: "Lifting to heaven holy hands which are kept unstained by anger and dissensions."

4. Should our pastor read his prayers?

That is between him and the Lord. Personally, I would rather a minister read a *meaningful* prayer than utter an extempore prayer that is shallow and routine. The prayers of many preachers are very predictable. My own practice was to think through my pulpit prayer on Saturday evening and write out key words and phrases to direct me. However, the danger here is that your pastoral prayer becomes what Spurgeon termed "an oblique sermon." (By the way, Spurgeon taught his pastoral students to prepare their pulpit prayers.)

The best preparation for public prayer is private prayer and meditation on God's Word. When the minister is in a truly spiritual frame of mind, the prayer will come, and the preparation will help to focus it on the requests that matter most. I have personally profited greatly from the reading of the prayers of great Christians, and I recommend it as a private devotional exercise.

5. What is a "litany" and how do we use it?

The word "litany" comes from the Greek and means "supplication." A litany is a prepared prayer offered by the minister, with the congregation responding with the same phrase at stated intervals. For example:

M: O Lord, we come as Your children, giving thanks for the gift of Your Word.
C: *We praise You, Lord, for Your Word.*
M: Your Word is a lamp to our feet and a light to our path.
C: *We praise You, Lord, for Your Word.*

Litanies are often used for the dedication of a church building, an organ, and so on. They may also be used for the confession of sin. I know of nothing unscriptural in the use of litanies (see Psalm 136), but we must always beware of empty routine. However, a well-planned litany can be very meaningful if a congregation is taught how to use it properly.

6. *Our pastor is getting into the habit of opening the service with a lot of banalities—the weather, what he did on Saturday, something that happened in Sunday school—and I think he is wrong. I like a worship service to start with a definite call to worship, not a weather report.*

In some congregations, it is difficult to make the transition between Sunday school and church; and often at the beginning of the service, people are moving around and there is noise. Some ministers take the first few minutes, while people are assembling, to share "family news" within the church and to welcome visitors, and so forth. Then, when things have calmed down, the worship begins.

The important thing is that *definite word is given that the worship service has begun.* It can be a signal from the organ or piano, or a song from the choir; it could even be a call to worship from the Scripture. Beyond that point, *nobody* should be doing anything else but worshiping God, and this applies especially to the worship leaders. I can never understand why the platform people must talk to each other and even be flippant with each other when they are supposed to be leading us in worship. They ought to be concentrating on worshiping God.

Worship must not be divorced from the realities of life—including the weather—but the focus of our attention should be on God. I prefer to open a service on a high and holy note of praise and adoration. The call to worship should center on God and His greatness, and the first hymn should be directed to Him in praise.

7. *I am a pastor, and when I went to school, we were not taught how to worship or how to lead worship. How do I sustain a worshipful atmosphere throughout a service?*

All of us are human, and it is impossible for human beings to operate at peak performance throughout an entire service of a hour or more in length. A famous movie producer once said that he wanted his films to start with an earthquake and then work up to a climax. You can do this with celluloid but not with congregations.

We should begin on a high note as we call the people to worship. The first hymn should lift their hearts to praise God, as once more they realize His greatness and glory. The first prayer should ask God for His help as the congregation worships. Psychological false fire will not last: we need the fire of the Spirit of God to warm our hearts and energize us as we worship.

The various elements of the worship service should be balanced: the prayers, the Scripture readings, the hymns, the sermon, and the offering. Personally, I dislike everything in a service to be devoted to the same theme, except on special occasions when the situation demands it (the ordaining of a minister, the sending out of a missionary, the recognition of a special day, and so forth). The worship leader must know the hymnal as well as he or she knows the Bible.

A worship service has a momentum of its own, and each service is different. You cannot sustain a high pitch of involvement or excitement without wearing out the people. A balanced service will have silence as well as speech and song, participation and rest, the spontaneous and the planned. A worship leader must be sensitive to the Spirit's leading and be willing to follow.

8. *Is there any place for humor in a service of worship?*

Sometimes you cannot help it! A worship leader with a good sense of humor can deal with awkward or embarrassing situations without destroying the atmosphere of the service. However, I would vote against forced or contrived humor that can only call attention to itself and distract from the true purpose of the service. The preacher or musician who "has to tell a joke" before ministering is, to me, definitely out of place.

Having said that, let me define the right use of humor in the service of God. Elbert Hubbard wrote, "A theologian who can not laugh is apt to explode—he is very dangerous." There is a difference between being serious and being solemn. In his Yale Lectures on Preaching, William Jewett Tucker said, "The humor of one preacher may be as reverent as the solemnity of another."

Anyone who has watched carefully either at a zoo or a shopping center knows that God has a sense of humor. There is a "holy joy" and even a "holy laughter" (Ps. 126:1-3) that can be born of the Spirit of God. Let it come unsought and it will glorify God. Manufacture it, and it will embarrass you.

9. *Ours is a small congregation and there is not a plentiful supply of musical talent. How do you worship God when the playing and singing are less than sensational?*

If the players and singers are doing their best, and seeking to do better, then God accepts their "sacrifices of praise" and so should we. Remember, our spiritual sacrifices are presented to God "through Jesus Christ," and that makes them acceptable (1 Pet. 2:5). Whenever I am listening to a below-average presentation, I imagine my Lord receiving it and presenting it to the Father; and that changes my attitude completely.

The worst thing you can do is to measure your music by what you hear at special concerts or over Christian media. Learn to appreciate the best, but (and I have said this before in these pages) do not become a religious highbrow who is above listening to anything but the best. I am afraid that some believers have become religious dilettantes who want to impress us with their highly developed sense of musical appreciation. Without love, however, they are just clanging gongs and cymbals

10. *I want to hitch hike on that last question. The Lord has given me a fine voice and I have been privileged to get considerable musical training. I attend a small church where there is not much musical talent. This means that I practice week by week in the choir with people who are really difficult to work with. I am tempted to go to a large church in our city where my musical ability would be put to better use. What do you think?*

Imagine what our Lord endured when He, the perfect Man, had to live with people like us here on earth! Even His own disciples often disappointed Him because of their immaturity and slowness of spiritual comprehension. True service must involve humility and sacrifice, according to Philippians 2.

Yes, the larger churches (with their bigger budgets) do attract people like you; but if all of you parade over to the big churches, what will happen to the other churches? I have pastored a small neighborhood church that was in the shadows of large churches, and I have also pastored large churches that helped to cast the shadows. But in both kinds of churches, my policy was to make sure the people were where God wanted them to be so that they might serve and glorify Him. On more than one occasion, I suggested to people that they stay in their own churches and not join our fellowship, because they were needed more there.

I can understand that a gifted musician might want a greater challenge and opportunity. I can also understand how frustrating it must be to practice weekly with less-talented people. However, keep in mind that you have a contribution to make right where you are. If you have a servant's heart, you will use your exceptional gifts to build others and not yourself.

Would it be possible for you to join a semiprofessional singing group and in that way find satisfaction? Perhaps you can even start one! There must be other people in your area who face a problem similar to yours.

Robert Murray McCheyne said, "God does not bless great talents. He blesses great likeness to Jesus." Be a blessing as you use your gifts and God will put you where He wants you.

11. In our church, somebody is "drafted" right before the service to read the Scripture. The pastor says he is led by the spirit when he chooses people, but after hearing the readings and the prayers I have my doubts. What do you suggest?

The public reading of the Word of God is too serious a matter to be left to unprepared people at the last minute. It was said that people learned more from Campbell Morgan's *reading* of Scripture than anybody else's *preaching* of Scripture. It must grieve the Spirit of God when the Holy Scriptures are read as carelessly as we hear them in some worship services.

If members of the congregation participate in the public reading of the Word, then they should be selected in advance, asked to prepare carefully, and coached by the pastor or an elder before the service. The Holy Spirit can lead us in our choices a month in advance just as easily as ten minutes in advance.

I recall with embarrassment the first time I read the Bible in the pulpit before a congregation. I had just been converted as a teenager, and some of the leaders in our little church wanted to encourage me. One Sunday morning, just before the service, the chairman of the church asked me to read the Scripture lesson, which happened to be Luke 3:1-6. Look it up and note all the unfamiliar names, plus that unfamiliar word "tetrarch" (which, by the way, is pronounced with either the long or short e). I stumbled through the passage and almost decided never to return to church. Fortunately, I got over it; but ever since, I have been sympathetic with people who are "drafted" to read Scripture at the last minute.

While I am on the subject, let me state my amazement that so many fundamental churches that defend the Word of God use it so little in their public services. About the only Scripture that is read is the text for the pastor's sermon, and yet we are commanded to "give attention to reading" (1 Tim. 4:13); this refers to the public reading of the Word of God in the congregation. Donald Guthrie claims that the Greek word *prosechō*, translated "give attention," means that there has been previous preparation in private.

Before leaving this matter, let me say that I lean strongly toward the view that we ought to have readings from the Old Testament, the Gospels, and the Epistles in our worship services. In the Jewish synagogue, they followed a lectionary (an order of selected readings), and this practice was adopted gradually by the church. The pastor who is sensitive to "the times and the seasons" as well as the needs of his congregation, need not feel imprisoned if he uses a lectionary to guide him. He can always make changes, but he ought to see to it that the Word of God is read in the public services.

One final suggestion: the pastor need not always do all the reading. He should use believers from the congregation, people who have been prepared in advance. I recall one service where a father, mother, and teenage daughter shared in the Scripture reading, making it a lovely family affair.

12. Must we always have a public invitation?

No, but we should always let lost sinners know what can be done if God's Spirit is speaking to their hearts. I like to have the congregation sing a closing hymn in response to the Word; although it need not be an "invitation hymn" as such, it can be used in that way if the Lord directs. Remember, we are worshiping God; and if our worship has been real and vital, the Spirit will have opportunity to speak to lost people. I have known lost people to trust Christ right in the middle of a service and never let us know until days later. Their experience was just as valid as if they had walked the aisle.

We must not make the invitation a test of orthodoxy or evangelistic zeal. There is more than one way to draw in the net. Not every baby is born in public.

13. Why must we keep learning new songs? I'm perfectly satisfied with the familiar ones I grew up on.

We might just as well ask, "Why must we keep buying new clothes?" Because we are growing and the old ones do not fit any more! If a church is growing in grace and knowledge, it must express that faith in new ways. This does not mean that we abandon the old songs, because they represent a rich heritage from which we can draw spiritual treasure. But a growing people cannot sing "Jesus Loves Me" every Sunday and have a full worship experience.

The important thing is to have standards for our music so that whether the song is old or new, we can determine its value. Some songs can be used at an informal Bible study that would not fit into a stated worship service. By having an occasional "singspiration" meeting, you can usually satisfy the members who have their favorites and want to sing them.

Be careful how you introduce new songs, even though the song may have been in the hymnals for a century. Be sure to explain why the song is meaningful to you or to the church, and always tie it to Scripture. Perhaps the background of the song would help to create interest among your people.

A vibrant congregation needs the continuity of the familiar as well as the challenge of the new. It takes both the minute hand and the hour hand to tell time on your watch, and yet one moves faster than the other.

14. From reading Christian magazines, I note that there is a growing trend toward "liturgical tradition" and that some evangelical leaders are abandoning the "free church" worship and promoting ritual. How do you feel about this?

I think that we are going to see more and more people in our fundamental churches do the same thing. They will no doubt give different reasons, and some of them may not even know why they are doing it. My own feeling is that many people have become weary of the shallow worship experience that some churches provide. These people are growing in the Lord and want something with more substance to it. Unfortunately, some of them put aesthetics ahead of doctrine and end up in churches whose doctrines may not agree with theirs. Having known nothing but plain "free church" worship all their life, they are impressed with the colorful ritual even though they may not understand the theology or tradition behind it.

Please understand that I am not condemning any particular Christian communion or approach to worship. All I am saying is that when good and godly people no longer feel at home, it may be an indication that *something is missing at home*. The evangelical churches need to take a new interest in worship and make sure that the worship experiences they provide are biblical, enriching, and satisfying to the whole man.

Each of us has different needs at different stages in our life. As we grow in our knowledge of Christ and His Word, we must have opportunity to express ourselves in more mature ways. We must be sure that, if we do change churches, our move is a mark of maturity, not childishness, and that we are fully convinced in our own mind and not merely influenced by some temporary problem or desire. Worship is a serious thing, and we dare not "choose churches" the way people select stores or restaurants.

15. In his book Preaching and Preachers, *Dr. Martyn Lloyd-Jones warns that preaching declines whenever there is "an increase in the formal element in the service." Please comment.*

The late Dr. Lloyd-Jones was my friend and I would not want to debate him since he cannot appear to defend himself or explain further what he meant. Perhaps the weight of his criticism should be on the word *formal*. When liturgy becomes an end in itself, then it certainly would minimize preaching, and I would oppose such a trend. It is difficult to know, however, whether "ritualism" is the cause or the result of poor preaching. Perhaps both are involved.

There are not many men who can preach like Dr. Lloyd-Jones and hold a congregation week after week with detailed expositions of the Scriptures. I always had the impression that "The Doctor" thought *anybody* could do what he did!

I consider preaching an act of worship, so there really is no competition between "ceremony" (the liturgy) and preaching. Both are a part of worship, and both have their place of ministry. I can see where a strong ritualist would be prone to minimize preaching, and this would be a grave mistake. It is a matter of balance. Often when a church has a "great preacher" in the pulpit, the "worship" part of the service is looked upon as "preliminaries to prepare the heart for the Word," and this is a concept I disagree with. The next step is to worship the preacher, and that is idolatry.

16. If I understand your concept of preaching, you are against outlines. Most of the preachers I have heard could use more organization in their messages, not less!

No, you have misunderstood me; I apologize for not making it clearer. A sermon must have some kind of logical development or it can never be communicated to others. What bothers me is that too often the preacher so emphasizes the outline (especially if it is alliterated) that the people miss the message. Furthermore, too often we preachers force the Scriptures into some artificial analysis in order to have "a good outline." We are so outline-conscious that we forget why we are preaching. The content of the message is important, but so also is the intent.

Suppose my wife and I invited you over for dinner, and throughout the meal kept telling you what the menu is, the order in which the dishes were served, the vitamin and mineral content of each dish, and so on. My guess is that you would get tired of that kind of conversation and say, "All of that is fine, but just let me enjoy the meal."

To continue the analogy: the fact that my wife sets the table in a beautiful manner, has everything arranged in order, and serves the food graciously, does make for a more enjoyable meal. So with homiletics. Have good food, set the table in an orderly and attractive manner, but please do not keep talking about it!

Not every preacher is an "outliner." Every preacher ought to be organized in his thinking and preparing, and orderly in his presentation, but he must not make an idol of his outlines. (Remember Campbell Morgan's little fire.)

17. I am confused about this matter of symbols. I always thought symbolism ended at the Crucifixion. Why use symbols in worship today?

A symbol is that which represents something else and helps us to understand it more and more. Symbols are universal. In the Bible, a yoke is a symbol; it conveys many lessons to us as we think about it. A dove is a symbol. "The seed is the word of God." The more you think about it, the more it says to you.

A sign simply points to something else and conveys information. For example, a skull and crossbones on a bottle is a sign of danger; a flashing red light means "Stop!" Nobody meditates on the skull or the flashing light. But while a sign merely conveys information, a symbol conveys insight and inspiration.

The Bible uses symbolism from beginning to end. Jesus is the Lamb of God. Satan is a roaring lion. The church is a flock of sheep. The Bible is a two-edged sword. It is impossible to understand the Bible apart from these symbols. There is symbolism in baptism and in the Lord's Supper. There is symbolism in a wedding ceremony (the lifting of the veil, the exchange of rings, the lighting of a "unity candle," and so forth), and in a funeral service (dropping flowers or dirt on the casket, "planting" the body in the ground like a seed, and so forth).

Symbols have the advantage of not only instructing our minds, but also stirring our hearts—and we need emotion in our worship. Furthermore, each individual perceives the symbol differently, depending on his or her spiritual maturity and personal experience. Symbols reach different people at different levels, something a mere lecture cannot always do.

The most nonritualistic church still has its symbolism, both by what is absent and what is present. The design of the building, the arrangement of the furniture in the room, the kind of people who participate in the service, even the order of the service, all have symbolic meaning. In other words, we cannot avoid symbolism.

Churches that would never permit candles on the Communion table will often have beautiful flowers there, and the flowers preach a symbolic message just as much as the candles. Pastors who will not permit candles on Sunday morning will permit dozens of them at weddings. Church members who have lovely Christian mottoes on their walls at home will not permit colorful banners on the walls of the church sanctuary. Even colors can be used symbolically; in fact, most churches that follow the Christian Year change the "altar colors" from season to season.

A large, open Bible on the Communion Table is a symbol that tells the worshipers that God's Word is central in the church. A world map in the narthex announces that the church family has a concern for a lost world.

Now, symbolism can be overdone; and if we are not careful, it can be misunderstood. New Christians must be taught the meanings of these symbols so that they can participate in worship with understanding. Moreover, our symbolism must be solidly based on Scripture so that it has orthodox theological content. There is a difference between sanctified imagination and mere fantasy! A friend of mine once spent an entire lunch hour trying to convince me that using hamburgers and Coca-Cola for the Lord's Supper would be more meaningful to people today than using bread and wine!

I suppose personal taste enters in as well. Some people are "Puritanical" by nature and resist anything that even hints of symbolism or ritual. We respect their feelings so long as they understand that these are *feelings* and not *convictions*, and that they are not called of God to try to convert the rest of us. God has chosen to use symbolism to convey spiritual truth, and it can be used in that way today. To worship God "in spirit" does not mean we jettison everything sensory. As Martin Luther said, God gave us five senses and we ought to use all of them in worshiping Him.

18. Is it right to get our worship pattern from the Old Testament? As Christians, should we not focus primarily on what the New Testament teaches?

God changes His dispensations but not His principles. Old Testament saints were saved by faith (read Hebrews 11) and they lived and worshiped by faith. While the externals may be different, the spiritual essentials are the same. The only Bible the early church had was the Old Testament, and the Spirit was able to use it to guide the church in their worship.

The first Christians were Jews, and they continued some of the practices found in the temple and synagogue. When the Gentiles came into the church, they no doubt enriched the worship with whatever expressions of worship were indigenous to them and approved by the Lord.

In one of the churches I pastored, one Sunday morning we opened the service with a fanfare of praise by a brass quartet. After the service, one of the long-time members accosted me with, "What kind of opening was that? Just a lot of noise! Who ever heard of a New Testament church starting a service like that!" I gently reminded her that Psalm 150:5 told us to praise God with loud and high-sounding cymbals—but we had not done that yet!

Please do not get the idea that Old Testament worship was loud, dramatic, and exuberant, while New Testament worship was quiet, laid-back, and timid. I doubt that the Jewish believers suddenly changed their whole approach to worship when they trusted Christ. They continued to use the psalms (1 Cor. 14:26), and the worship expressions in the psalms are anything but timid!

The Old Testament legal ceremonies were fulfilled in Christ, so we do not repeat them today. But I see no reason why we must make an artificial distinction between "Old Testament worship" and "New Testament worship" when we see no such distinction in Scripture. That God revealed Himself and His requirements for blessing over a period of years is clear. His methods of working changed from age to age, but the principles of the spiritual life do not change. I take it that this includes worship.

19. I must confess that I am a bit worried about that word mystic. *Are Christians supposed to be mystics?*

No need to be worried! A mystic is a person who believes that we can experience God personally, and that the material world is not the real world and the spiritual world is what counts. A mystic sees God in everything around him and seeks to know God better and become more like Him.

Now, there are different kinds of mystics. A Christian mystic bases his belief and experience on the Word of God. He or she will not bypass Jesus Christ and Scripture. There are schools of mysticism today that are definitely unbiblical in their approach, and you want to avoid them.

There is no question that the great saints of Bible days enjoyed this mystical experience with God, sometimes paying a great price to have it. Here and there, down through the centuries, great mystics have emerged and called us back to the spiritual priorities of life. Some of them wrote books that are still meaningful to us.

You may not realize it, but many of our familiar worship hymns give expression to a mystical experience. "Jesus, lover of my soul/Let me to Thy bosom fly" is a mystical expression. "There is a place of quiet rest/Near to the heart of God" is another. One of the clearest expressions of Christian mysticism in a song is "I Am His and He Is Mine" by George Wade Robinson. Another is "Jesus, I Am Resting, Resting" by Jean S. Pigott.

A mystic is not satisfied with proper doctrinal formulas or traditional church ceremonies. He does not reject them, of course, but seeks to use them as pathways to God. He seeks a satisfying experience with God, whether it be love or fear, conviction or joy, quietness or a stirring for service. "My soul thirsts for God, for the living God!" is the evangelical mystic's expression of desire (Ps. 42:2).

I suppose the greatest exponent of Christian evangelical mysticism in recent years has been Dr. A. W. Tozer, whose books I have quoted often in these pages. *The Pursuit of God* is perhaps his best exposition of what he feels it means to be an evangelical mystic. He gives a concise explanation also in the introduction to his anthology, *The Christian Book of Mystical Verse*.

Dr. D. Martyn Lloyd-Jones once told me that he and Tozer, while sharing in a Bible conference, discussed their thinking about the church and the Christian life. They came to the conclusion that they pretty much agreed. Tozer had come by way of the mystics and Lloyd-Jones by way of the Puritans, and yet they were of one mind on the essentials.

If you want an introduction to Tozer's writings, see my anthology *The Best of A. W. Tozer* (published by Baker Book House).

20. You did not say much about family worship in the home. Any suggestions here?

It must be regular, systematic, and flexible. Mother and father must have their own personal "quiet time" before they attempt to lead their children. One of the purposes for a family devotional time is to teach the children how to have their own quiet time and to help to develop in them a desire for a daily fellowship with God.

There must be variety and flexibility. As the children mature, the older ones can assist in the reading and praying. While it must not be a "fun time"(although there is nothing wrong with a good laugh), it should be enjoyable. Our practice was to gear the reading to the youngest member of the family, whose attention span was much shorter than ours.

We wore out two copies of Ken Taylor's *Bible Stories With Pictures for Little Eyes*, and now our children are using it with our grandchildren! We tried to provide age-graded devotional material for each child as he or she matured in years and in the faith. This was not always easy. We encouraged them to read systematically in the Word, to meditate on it, and to pray.

Each family must determine when is the best time for the family altar. At one stage in our lives, after breakfast was the ideal time. Later, with changing school schedules, it was more convenient immediately after supper. There were some days when the schedule fell apart and we had no devotional time at all with the children. But we did not feel guilty; we just picked it up the next day and kept on going.

By the way, when you and the family are driving down the highway, you have a wonderful opportunity for an impromptu family altar. (If you are the driver, be sure to *watch* and pray!) The spontaneous devotional times can carry more power than some of our carefully prepared sessions.

Our children need to be taught what worship is. They will see in us, the parents, what God is really like. If Dad or Mom piously goes through a family devotional time, but then does not live like a Christian the rest of the day, more harm than good will come from the family altar. God often gives us parents opportunities *during the day* to practice what we talked about at the family altar, and we must not waste these opportunities.

Vitality—variety—spontaneity—flexibility: those would be the characteristics of a successful family altar.

21. *Nobody today seems satisfied with the church, and each leader has a different solution to the problem. How far back must we go into church history before we can find the approach that will work today?*

You are right: every preacher or writer who critiques the church wants us to "go back" and recover something that the church has lost. Some of the "superaggressive churches" and their leaders want us to go back to the days of Billy Sunday and D. L. Moody, when the emphasis was on evangelism. Dr. Lloyd-Jones urged us to go further back than that, to the Puritans. "The sooner we forget the nineteenth century and go back to the eighteenth, and even further to the seventeenth and sixteenth, the better!" is what he said.

Others insist that we return to Luther and the Reformation. Another group wants us to return to the Eastern Orthodox Church, and another to the church of the fourth century. It always seems that *the past* was better than the present.

A journalist accused Billy Graham of setting the church back two hundred years. Mr. Graham said that if that were true, he considered himself a failure; because he really wanted to set the church back two thousand years, back to the book of Acts!

We can learn—and we *should* learn—from every age of church history; but we must not make any one age so ideal that we begin to imitate it. "Do not say, 'Why were the former days better than these?' For you do not inquire wisely concerning this" (Eccles. 7:10).

It appears that during each age of church history, God enabled the church to recover some lost truth. Luther recovered justification by faith and the priesthood of believers. Wesley recovered evangelism and holy living. Today, our charismatic friends have encouraged us to get acquainted with the Holy Spirit of God. Each age learned something and lost something; so we should be wise and profit from their gains and beware of their losses. But to make any one age the final example of what God can do would be dangerous. Even the apostolic age, which is probably our best example, had its weaknesses and problems.

Instruction and inspiration—yes! Imitation—no.

APPENDIX 2 *An informal bibliography*

Along with the books mentioned in the footnotes, the serious student of worship should find the following volumes helpful. The fact that I have listed a book here, or quoted from one in the text, does not mean I am endorsing all that the author believes or has written. (Those marked * are no longer in print but may be found in your church or other library.)

Allen, Ronald, and Borror, Gordon. *Worship: Rediscovering the Missing Jewel.* Portland, OR: Multnomah Press, 1982.

Baxter, J. Sidlow. *Majesty: The God You Should Know.* San Bernardino, CA: Here's Life, 1984.

———. *Rethinking Our Priorities.* Grand Rapids: Zondervan Publishing House, 1974.*

Cullman, Oscar. *Early Christian Worship.* Philadelphia: Westminster Press, 1978.

Dobson, J. O. *Worship.* London: S.C.M. Press, 1941.*

Flynn, Leslie. *Worship: Together We Celebrate.* Wheaton, IL: Victor Books, 1983.

Gibbs, Alfred D. *Worship, The Christian's Highest Occupation.* Kansas City, KS: Walterick Publications, n.d.

Hahn, Ferdinand. *The Worship of the Early Church.* Philadelphia: Fortress Press, 1973.

Happold, Frank C. *Mysticism.* New York: Penguin Books, 1963.

Hustad, Donald P. *Jubilate! Church Music in the Evangelical Tradition.* Carol Stream, IL: Hope Publishing Co., 1981.

MacArthur, John. *The Ultimate Priority.* Chicago: Moody Press, 1983.

Martin, Ralph P. *The Worship of God.* Grand Rapids: W. B. Eerdmans, 1982.

———. *Worship in the Early Church.* Grand Rapids: W. B. Eerdmans, 1964.

Maxwell, William D. *An Outline of Christian Worship.* New York: Oxford University Press, 1936.

———. *Concerning Worship.* New York: Oxford University Press, 1948.

Merton, Thomas. *New Seeds of Contemplation.* New York: New Directions Books, 1972.

Minear, Paul. *Images of the Church in the New Testament*. Philadelphia: Westminster Press, 1970.

Morey, Robert A. *Worship Is All of Life*. Camp Hill, PA: Christian Publications, 1984.

O'Brien, Elmer. *Varieties of Mystic Experience*. New York: New American Library, Mentor Books, 1964.*

Ortlund, Anne. *Up With Worship*. Glendale, CA: Regal Books, 1982.

Rayburn, Robert G. *O Come, Let Us Worship*. Grand Rapids: Baker Book House, 1980.*

Saliers, Don E. *Worship and Spirituality*. Philadelphia: Westminster Press, 1984.

Sheppard, Lancelot, ed. *True Worship*. Baltimore: The Helicon Press, 1963.*

Underhill, Evelyn. *The Evelyn Underhill Reader*. Compiled by Thomas S. Kepler. New York: Abingdon, 1962.*

Ware, Timothy. *The Orthodox Church*. Harmondsworth: Penguin Books, 1963.

Webber, Robert. *Worship Is a Verb*. Waco, TX: Word Books, 1985.

———. *Worship Old & New*. Grand Rapids: Zondervan Publishing House, 1982.

White, James F. *Introduction to Christian Worship*. Nashville: Abingdon Press, 1980.

Wiersbe, Warren W. *The Best of A. W. Tozer*. Eastbourne: Kingsway Publications, 1983.

Willimon, William H. *Preaching and Leading Worship*. Philadelphia: Westminster Press, 1984.

———. *Worship as Pastoral Care*. Nashville: Abingdon Press, 1979.

APPENDIX 3 *Notes*

CHAPTER 1

1. G. Campbell Morgan, *The Westminster Pulpit* (London: Pickering and Inglis, n.d.), vol. 8, p. 248.
2. A. W. Tozer, *What Ever Happened To Worship?* (Camp Hill, PA: Christian Publications, 1985, published in the UK by STL/Kingsway), p. 12.

CHAPTER 2

3. Evelyn Underhill, *Worship* (London: Nisbet and Co., Ltd., 1936), p. 61.
4. William Temple, *Readings in St. John's Gospel*, First Series (London: Macmillan and Co., 1939), p. 68.
5. A. W. Tozer, *Man, The Dwelling Place of God* (Harrisburg, PA: Christian Publications, 1966), p. 57.
6. Alfred North Whitehead, *Science and the Modern World* (New York: The Free Press, 1967), p. 12.
7. D. Martyn Lloyd-Jones, *Faith on Trial* (Grand Rapids: W. B. Eerdmans, 1965, published in the UK by IVP), p. 43.
8. G. Campbell Morgan, *The Letters of Our Lord* (London: Pickering & Inglis, n.d.), p. 72.
9. A. W. Tozer, *The Root of the Righteous* (Harrisburg, PA: Christian Publications, 1955), p. 38.
10. G. Campbell Morgan, *The Acts of the Apostles* (London: Pickering & Inglis, 1924).

CHAPTER 3

11. Albert W. Palmer in *Paths to the Presence of God* quoted in Thomas S. Kepler, comp., *The Fellowship of the Saints* (New York: Abingdon-Cokesbury, 1948), p. 680.
12. John Charles Ryle, *Knots Untied* (London: James Clark and Co., Ltd., 1964), p. 234.

13. John R. W. Stott, *Your Mind Matters* (Downers Grove, IL: InterVarsity Press, 1972, published in the UK by IVP), p. 32.

14. Washington Gladden, *The Christian Way*, quoted in Kepler, *Fellowship of the Saints*, p. 577.

CHAPTER 4

15. William Quayle, *The Pastor-Preacher*, ed. Warren W. Wiersbe (Grand Rapids: Baker Book House, 1979), p. 73.

16. Quote from *The International Thesaurus of Quotations*, comp. Rhonda Thomas Tripp (New York: Crowell, 1970), p. 704.

17. *Ibid.*

18. *Ibid.*, p. 471.

19. T. F. Torrance, *God and Rationality*, quoted in Geoffrey Wainwright, *Doxology: The Praise of God in Worship, Doctrine, and Life* (New York: Oxford University Press, 1980), p. 437.

20. Quoted in Sam Keen, *Apology for Wonder* (New York: Harper & Row, 1969), p. 42.

21. Quoted in Ray Summers, *The Secret Sayings of the Living Jesus* (Waco, TX: Words Books, 1968), p. 21.

CHAPTER 5

22. C. H. Spurgeon, *The Early Years* (London: The Banner of Truth Trust, 1962), p. 390.

23. *The Confessions of St. Augustine*, in *A Select Library of the Nicene and Post-Nicene Fathers*, vol. 1, first series (Grand Rapids: W. B. Eerdmans, reprint 1979), p. 466.

24. Underhill, *Worship*, p. 174.

25. Robert N. Linscott, ed., *Selected Poems and Letters of Emily Dickenson* (Garden City, NY: Anchor Books), p. 7.

26. C. S. Lewis, *The Screwtape Letters* (New York: The Macmillan Publishing Co., 1962, published in the UK by Fount), pp. 21, 22.

27. Quoted in *The New Dictionary of Thoughts*, comp. Tryon Edwards, rev. Catrevas, Edwards & Browns (Cincinnati: Standard Book Co., 1964), p. 292.

28. *The Complete Essays and Other Writings of Ralph Waldo Emerson*, ed. Brooks Atkinson (New York: The Modern Library, 1950), p. 3.

29. *Congregational Praise* (Independent Press, Ltd., for the Congregational Church in England and Wales, tenth impression, 1967), p. 27.

30. Leon Morris, *The Cross in the New Testament* (Grand Rapids: W. B. Eerdmans, 1965, published in the UK by Paternoster), p. 5.

31. D. Martyn Lloyd-Jones, *Faith on Trial*, pp. 89, 90.

32. *Congregational Praise*, p. 73.

33. A. W. Tozer, comp., *The Christian Book of Mystical V* burg, PA: Christian Publications, 1963), pp. 114, 115.

CHAPTER 6

34. The expositional outline is adapted from my book *Meet Yourself in the Psalms* (1983), chapter 2, and is used by permission of the publishers, Victor Books, Wheaton, IL.

CHAPTER 7

35. Jonathan Edwards, *Selected Writings of Jonathan Edwards*, ed. Harold P. Simpson (New York: Frederick Ungar Publishing Co., 1970), p. 40.

36. Matthew Henry, *Commentary on the Whole Bible* (Old Tappan, NJ: Fleming H. Revell, n.d.), vol. 3, comments on Ecclesiastes 5:1, 2.

37. Frank S. Mead, ed., *The Encyclopedia of Religious Quotations* (Old Tappan, NJ: Fleming H. Revell, 1965), p. 201.

38. *Ibid.*, p. 464.

39. Alexander Maclaren, *Expositions of Holy Scripture* (Grand Rapids: Baker Book House, reprint 1971), vol. 5, p. 22.

40. Merrill C. Tenney, *Interpreting Revelation* (Grand Rapids: W. B. Eerdmans, 1957), p. 36.

CHAPTER 8

41. *Congregational Praise*, p. 240.

42. Underhill, *Worship*, p. 84.

43. John Calvin, *The Institutes of the Christian Religion*, ed. John T. McNeil (Philadelphia: Westminster Press, 1960, published in the UK by Banner of Truth Trust), vol. 2, p. 1024.

CHAPTER 9

44. A. W. Tozer, *The Divine Conquest* (Harrisburg, PA: Christian Publications, 1950), p. 90.

45. A. W. Tozer, *The Pursuit of God* (Harrisburg, PA: Christian Publications, 1950), p. 11.

46. Tozer, *Root of the Righteous*, p. 81.

47. Quoted in Kepler, *Fellowship of the Saints*, p. 469.

48. Charles H. Spurgeon, *Lectures To My Students* (London: Marshall, Morgan & Scott, reprinted 1965), p. 68.

CHAPTER 10

49. Ryle, *Knots Untied*, pp. 226–230.

50. Oswald Chambers, *Shade of His Hand* (Fort Washington, PA: Christian Literature Crusade, 1973), p. 52.

51. A. W. Tozer, *God Tells the Man Who Cares* (Harrisburg, PA: Christian Publications, 1970), p. 11.

52. Leon Morris, *The Gospel According to John* in The New International Commentary on the New Testament (Grand Rapids: W. B. Eerdmans, 1971), p. 378. Dr. Morris's treatment of the sacramental element in John 6 is masterful.

CHAPTER 11

53. J. I. Packer and R. J. Coates, *Beyond the Battle for the Bible* (Westchester, IL: Crossway Books, 1980), p. 84.

54. *Ibid.*, p. 67.

55. *Ibid.*, p. 85.

56. Sermon by G. Campbell Morgan in *Great Sermons on The Resurrection of Christ*, comp. Wilbur M. Smith (Grand Rapids: Baker Book House, 1964), pp. 104, 105.

57. Northrop Frye, *The Educated Imagination* (Bloomington, IN: Indiana University Press, 1969), p. 22.

58. John Harries, *Campbell Morgan: The Man and His Ministry* (New York: Fleming H. Revell, 1930), p. 46.

59. Frank Cairns, *The Prophet of the Heart* (London: Hodder & Stoughton, 1934), pp. 56, 57.

60. *Ibid.*, pp. 63, 64.

61. A. W. Tozer, *Of God and Men* (Harrisburg, PA: Christian Publications, 1960), p. 26.

62. Tozer, *The Root of the Righteous*, p. 55.

CHAPTER 12

63. Frank C. Senn, *Christian Worship and Its Cultural Setting* (Philadelphia; Fortress Press, 1983), p. 75.

64. Francis A. Schaeffer, *Art and The Bible* (Downers Grove, IL: Inter-Varsity Press, 1973), p. 7.

65. Calvin, *The Institutes*, vol. 1, p. 112.

66. *Ibid.*

67. Quoted in Kepler, *Fellowship of the Saints*, p. 264.

68. Irwin Edman, *Arts and the Man* (New York: W. W. Norton, 1939), p. 12.

69. Spurgeon, *C. H. Spurgeon's Autobiography*, vol. 3 (London: Passmore and Alabaster, 1899), pp. 327, 328.

70. Edman, *Arts and the Man*, p. 121.

71. Richard Allen Bodey, "The Sacrifice of Song," in *Voices*, vol. 11, no. 3 (1985), published by Trinity Evangelical Divinity School, Deerfield, IL.

72. C. H. Macintosh, *Notes on Genesis* (New York: Loizeaux Brothers, Inc., 1948), p. 76.

73. John Calvin, *Commentary Upon the Book of Genesis* (Grand Rapids: Baker Book House, reprint 1981), p. 218.

74. Quoted in *What Luther Says*, comp. Ewald M. Plass, vol. 2 (Saint Louis: Concordia Publishing House, 1959), p. 982.

75. *Ibid.*, p. 980.

76. James Boswell, *The Life of Samuel Johnson*, "Everyman's Library" edition (New York: E. P. Dutton, 1973), vol. 2, p. 144.

77. Harold M. Best, "Christian Responsibility in Music," in *Christian Imagination*, edited by Leland Ryken (Grand Rapids: Baker Book House, 1981), p. 407.

78. Schaeffer, *Art and the Bible*, p. 51.

79. For an example of this kind of preaching, see *Scriptures That Sing* by Warren W. Wiersbe, published by Back to the Bible, Lincoln, NE 68501.

80. Senn, *Christian Worship*, p. 38.

81. *Ibid.*, p. 62.

CHAPTER 13

82. Charles H. Spurgeon, *The Treasury of David*, vol. 7 (Grand Rapids: Baker Book House, 1977), p. 439.

83. Temple, *Readings in St. John's Gospel*, Second Series (London: Macmillan & Co., 1940), p. 209.

84. There are numerous books available on Satanology, but, oddly enough, none of them deals in depth with Satan and worship. Along with the standard systematic theology texts, you may want to consult: *The Invisible War* by Donald Grey Barnhouse (Zondervan, 1980); *The Adversary* and *Overcoming the Adversary* by Mark I. Bubeck (Moody Press, 1975 and 1984); *Angels, Elect and Evil* by C. Fred Dickason (Moody Press, 1975); *I Believe in Satan's Downfall* by Michael Green (Eerdmans, 1981); *Your Adversary the Devil* by J. Dwight Pentecost (Zondervan, 1976); *Demons in the World Today* by Merrill F. Unger (Tyndale, 1980); *The Strategy of Satan* by Warren W. Wiersbe (Tyndale, 1979).

CHAPTER 14

85. *The Ante-Nicene Fathers*, vol. 1 (Grand Rapids: W. B. Eerdmans, reprint 1979), p. 55.

86. Michael Green, *I Believe in Satan's Downfall* (Grand Rapids: W. B. Eerdmans, 1981, published in the UK by Hodder & Stoughton), p. 248.

87. Quoted in *A Reader's Notebook*, comp. Gerald Kennedy (New York: Harper, 1953), p. 324.

88. Frederick W. Robertson, *Sermons*, vol. 5 (London: Kegan Paul, Trench, Trubner & Co., 1900), p. 122.

Worship

by Graham Kendrick

Hymns—choruses; silence—noise; kneeling—dancing; liturgy—freedom.

Whatever our personal preferences in worship, this book sets out to discover what *God* is looking for, as our worship is primarily for him. What part should worship play in our lives? And how does this affect the way we relate together as God's people?

Whether you are a leader of worship or see yourself as playing a more passive role, this book is designed to help you experience greater depth and meaning in your highest calling—to worship the living God.

GRAHAM KENDRICK has had many years' experience of leading worship in both small and large Christian gatherings. He is widely acknowledged as one of Britain's leading singer-songwriters, being well known for his many songs of praise and worship.

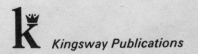

Kingsway Publications

Whatever Happened to Worship?

by A. W. Tozer

This is the book A. W. Tozer intended to write next. Now, more than twenty years after he was called home to heaven, it is available—compiled from tapes of sermons preached to his congregations in Toronto.

'True worship,' says Tozer, 'is to be so personally and hopelessly in love with God, that the idea of a transfer of affection never even remotely exists.'

Published jointly
with STL Books

Kingsway Publications